Lecture Notes of the Institute for Computer Sciences, Social Informatics and Telecommunications Engineering

324

More information about this series at http://www.springer.com/series/8197

Der-Jiunn Deng · Ai-Chun Pang ·
Chun-Cheng Lin (Eds.)

Smart Grid and Internet of Things

Third EAI International Conference, SGIoT 2019
TaiChung, Taiwan, December 5–6, 2019
Proceedings

Springer

Editors
Der-Jiunn Deng
National Changhua University of Education
Changhua City, Taiwan

Ai-Chun Pang
National Taiwan Normal University
Taipei, Taiwan

Chun-Cheng Lin
Department of Industrial Engineering
and Management
National Chiao Tung University
Hsinchu, Taiwan

ISSN 1867-8211　　　　　　　　ISSN 1867-822X　(electronic)
Lecture Notes of the Institute for Computer Sciences, Social Informatics
and Telecommunications Engineering
ISBN 978-3-030-49609-8　　　　　ISBN 978-3-030-49610-4　(eBook)
https://doi.org/10.1007/978-3-030-49610-4

This Springer imprint is published by the registered company Springer Nature Switzerland AG
The registered company address is: Gewerbestrasse 11, 6330 Cham, Switzerland

Preface

We are delighted to introduce the proceedings of the third edition of the European Alliance for Innovation (EAI) International Conference on Smart Grid and Internet of Things (SGIoT 2019). This year, the conference took place at the Windsor Hotel in Taichung, on November 28, 2019. SGIoT provides an opportunity for researchers, developers, and practitioners from around the world to connect and discuss recent findings in the emerging areas of Smart Grids and the Internet of Things. The technical program of SGIoT 2019 consisted of 10 full papers in oral presentation sessions at the main conference tracks.

Coordination with the steering chairs, Imrich Chlamtac, Xudong Wang, and Der-Jiunn Deng was essential for the success of the conference. We sincerely appreciate their constant support and guidance. It was also a great pleasure to work with such an excellent Organizing Committee and we thank them for their hard work in organizing and supporting the conference. In particular, the Technical Program Committee (TPC), led by our TPC co-chair Rung-Shiang Cheng, who completed the peer-review process of technical papers and made a high-quality technical program. We are also grateful to conference manager Lukas Skolek for his support and all the authors who submitted their papers to the SGIoT 2019 conference and workshops.

We strongly believe that the SGIoT conference provides a good forum for all researcher, developers, and practitioners to discuss all science and technology aspects that are relevant to wireless networks. We also expect that the future SGIoT conference will be as successful and stimulating, as indicated by the contributions presented in this volume.

April 2020

Der-Jiunn Deng
Ai-Chun Pang
Chun-Cheng Lin

Organization

Steering Committee

Xudong Wang   Shanghai Jiao Tong University, China
Der-Jiunn Deng   National Changhua University of Education, Taiwan

Organizing Committee

General Chair

Der-Jiunn Deng   National Changhua University of Education, Taiwan

General Co-chair

Ai-Chun Pang   National Taiwan University, Taiwan

TPC Chair and Co-chair

Chun-Cheng Lin   National Chiao Tung University, Taiwan
Rung-Shiang Cheng   Overseas Chinese University, Taiwan

Sponsorship and Exhibit Chair

Viviane Su   Institute for Information Industry, Taiwan

Local Chairs

Shin-Ming Cheng   National Taiwan University of Science
                                   and Technology, Taiwan
Hui Hsin Chin   Overseas Chinese University, Taiwan

Workshops Chair

Bo Li   Northwestern Polytechnical University, China

Publicity and Social Media Chairs

Anthony Y. Chang   Overseas Chinese University, Taiwan
Chi-Han Chen   Overseas Chinese University, Taiwan

Publications Chair

Yu-Liang Liu   Overseas Chinese University, Taiwan

Web Chair

Chien-Liang Chen   Overseas Chinese University, Taiwan

Technical Program Committee

Rung-Shiang Cheng	Overseas Chinese University, Taiwan
Chien-Liang Chen	Overseas Chinese University, Taiwan
Yu-Liang Liu	Overseas Chinese University, Taiwan
Chun-Hsien Sung	Overseas Chinese University, Taiwan
Jen-En Huang	Overseas Chinese University, Taiwan
Lung-Ping Hung	National Taipei University of Nursing and Health Sciences, Taiwan
Ding-Jung Chiang	Taipei Chengshih University of Science and Technology, Taiwan

Contents

Smart Grid and Internet of Things

Flag-Assisted Early Release of RRC Scheme for Power Saving in NB-IoT System

Hui-Ling Chang, Chung-Ying Hsieh, and Meng-Hsun Tsai[⊠] iD

National Cheng Kung University, Tainan, Taiwan
momo@imslab.csie.ncku.edu.tw, P76054290@mail.ncku.edu.tw,
tsaimh@csie.ncku.edu.tw

Abstract. As the 5G standard is about to be completed, the IoT applications will have the unprecedented development. Massive and various IoT devices sense and interact with the environment. Most of those devices are battery-powered and some of them are deployed at inaccessible locations, so how to reduce the power consumption is a critical issue. 3GPP proposed eDRX and two transport optimization mechanisms to help devices reduce power consumption. In this paper, based on the CP CIoT EPS Optimization, a flag-assisted Early Release of RRC scheme is proposed. The message flow is modified to make IoT devices enter RRC_IDLE early. The result shows that the flag-assisted Early Release of RRC can help IoT devices save power further.

Keywords: NB-IoT · CP CIoT EPS Optimization · Power saving · eDRX

1 Introduction

As the Fifth Generation (5G) standard is about to be completed and the worldwide telecom operators have announced the commercial 5G would be launched between 2018 and 2022 [1], the Internet of Things (IoT) applications will have the unprecedented development. Cisco estimated that IoT connections will be more than 14.6 billion by 2022 [2]. In the near future, smart home, smart city, smart factory, smart mobility, health care, etc. will be realized in our daily life [3]. A variety of devices with sensor, actuator, or both have the ability to communicate with each other and interact with the environment. Most of the IoT applications are small data transmission services. The Third Generation Partnership Project (3GPP) proposed the Narrow-Band IoT (NB-IoT) as the radio access technology in 5G for the classic IoT model of static, low-data-rate, and delay-tolerant nodes. NB-IoT supports the network connection which characterizes massive connection, low cost, ultra-low power consumption, and coverage enhancement.

How to reduce the power consumption is always a critical issue, because a majority of IoT devices are battery-powered and some of them are deployed at

D.-J. Deng et al. (Eds.): SGIoT 2019, LNICST 324, pp. 3–15, 2020.
https://doi.org/10.1007/978-3-030-49610-4_1

inaccessible locations. Even though the battery of some devices, e.g. smart fitness band, can be replaced or charged easily, prolonging the battery life in order to reduce the charging frequency is still important due to the user friendliness. In terms of power efficiency, NB-IoT has targeted a ten-year battery life with the capacity of 5 Wh [4], which is a quite challenging goal.

To achieve this target, 3GPP introduced extended Discontinuous Reception (eDRX) in Release 13. In legacy LTE, the devices adopting DRX periodically sleep to turn off the radio module for the sake of saving power and wake up to monitor the Physical Downlink Control Channel (PDCCH). The substantial difference between DRX and eDRX is that the device adopting eDRX spends more time to stay in sleep period, which greatly reduces the power consumption. The maximum cycle length in idle mode DRX is only 2.56 s while the cycle length can be up to 2.91 h in NB-IoT eDRX mechanism [5].

Moreover, 3GPP also proposed two transport optimization mechanisms in Release 13 to reduce the signal transmission [6]. One is User Plane Cellular IoT Evolved Packet System (UP CIoT EPS) Optimization which allows user equipments (UEs) to reduce the bearer setup signal (i.e., Access Stratum (AS) security setup and Radio Resource Control (RRC) reconfiguration messages) after an initial RRC connection is established by suspending and resuming procedures. The other one is Control Plane (CP) CIoT EPS Optimization. Although CP is used to transmit the signal message, CP CIoT EPS Optimization makes the user data encapsulated in Non-Access Stratum (NAS) message. As a result, the UEs avoid AS security setup and the UP bearer establishment. By these optimizations, NB-IoT has the ability to efficiently support massive Machine-Type Communication (mMTC) and further reduce the power consumption. Since most applications of NB-IoT are small data transmission, establishing user plane is unnecessary. 3GPP also specifies that UEs adopting NB-IoT must support CP CIoT EPS Optimization, while UP CIoT EPS Optimization is optional. For convenience, CP CIoT EPS Optimization is called CP CIoT for short in the following content.

The analysis in [7] shows that compared to using conventional Service Request (SR) procedure, adopting CP CIoT increases the battery life up to five years. However, this procedure still can be improved. Although eDRX can be performed in both RRC_CONNECTED and RRC_IDLE states, the power consumption in the RRC_CONNECTED Sleep mode is 200 times higher than that in RRC_IDLE Standby mode [8]. Obviously, the devices should enter RRC_IDLE as soon as possible after they transport the data. Therefore, based on CP CIoT, we proposed flag-assisted Early Release of RRC (ER-RRC) scheme in this paper. The existing message flow is modified for the IoT devices to stay in RRC_IDLE state longer and further save more power.

In LTE/LTE-A, some literatures analyzed the trade-off between the power saving and the latency by tuning the DRX parameters and tried to optimize the parameter setting under different traffic models to save power [9,10]. In our previous work [11], Optimistic DRX (ODRX) was introduced to appropriately skip the short cycles, which results in extra 20% power saving with just about 70 ms extra delay. In NB-IoT, the power saving issue is still popular. The authors in [12] analyzed the trade-off between the tracking area update (TAU) cost and the paging cost, and then optimized the length of eDRX cycle. The signaling cost is mitigated so the processing power is also reduced. A prediction-based power saving mechanism is developed in [13] to allocate resource in advance by observing the uplink occurrence and processing delay. The device can send uplink data without a scheduling request. The transmission time is reduced and thus the power can be saved. A group-based DRX is introduced to provide better power saving for a large-scale NB-IoT system [14]. The group leader adopts the DRX scheme different from that of the group members. The leader wakes up more often than the members do to monitor the downlink channel. The power of total IoT devices in the whole system can be saved and the signaling congestion can be avoided.

To the best of authors' knowledge, no research focused on improving the message flow. In this paper, CP CIoT is enhanced to make IoT devices enter eDRX earlier. Consequently, more power can be saved.

The rest of this paper is organized as follows. In Sect. 2, CP CIoT is described in detail. The proposed ER-RRC scheme is elaborated in Sect. 3. We also proposed the analytical model to validate our simulation in Sect. 4. The performance evaluation is shown in Sect. 5. Finally, we made the conclusion in Sect. 6.

2   CP CIoT EPS Optimization

In this section, the procedure of data transport in CP CIoT is elaborated in detail. First of all, a new information element (IE) called Release Assistance Indication (RAI) is introduced for CP CIoT. When the devices intend to transmit data, RAI can be included in NAS message to indicate that no further uplink (UL) or downlink (DL) data subsequent to this UL data is expected, or only a single DL data (e.g. a response to this UL data) is expected. In the first case, the RAI is set to one while in the second case, the RAI is set to two [15]. The message flows of mobile originated (MO) data transport with two RAI values are explained as follows.

Figure 1 illustrates the MO message flow with RAI = 1.

Step 0. The device is in RRC_IDLE. In this state, the device releases radio resource and performs eDRX. In each paging cycle, the device wakes up for only 1 ms to monitor the PDCCH [16].

Steps 1–2. The device performs the random access procedure to inform the evolved node B (eNB) its transmission request.

Steps 3–5. The device establishes a RRC connection. In RRC Connection Setup Complete message, the data and RAI value (i.e., RAI = 1) are included in the NAS PDU.

Step 6. The eNB relays the NAS PDU in S1-AP Initial UE message to the Mobility Management Entity (MME). Note that the eNB cannot retrieve information from NAS message.

Step 7. The MME checks the integrity of the NAS PDU and decrypts the UL user data for further transmission.

Steps 8–11. The MME requests to re-activate the bearers for the device.

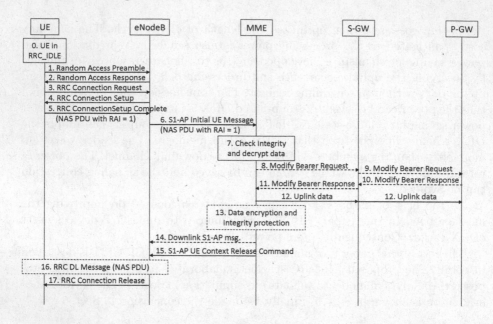

Fig. 1. MO data transport in CP CIoT EPS Optimization with RAI = 1

Step 12. The MME sends the UL user data to the Packet Data Network gateway (P-GW) via the Serving gateway (S-GW). Since RAI value is set to one, all application layer data exchanges are completed with this UL data. However, the MME may have pending data for the device. Therefore, the MME checks whether there is buffered data for the device or not. If not, the following **Step 13.**, **Step 14.**, and **Step 16.** are skipped.

Step 13. The MME is aware of pending MT data so it performs data encryption and protects the integrity of this data.

Step 14. The MT data is encapsulated in a NAS PDU and sent to the eNB.

Step 15. If the MME does not have pending data for the device, it immediately requests the eNB to release the connection after sending UL data to P-GW. If the MME has pending data for the device, it requests the eNB to release the connection right after sending DL S1-AP message.

Step 16. The eNB sends the RRC DL message with NAS PDU where the MT data is included to the device.

Step 17. The RRC connection between the device and the eNB is released. In the meantime, the S1 connection between the eNB and the MME for the device is also released. All the bearers are torn down. The eNB removes the context of the device and the device goes back to RRC_IDLE.

Figure 2 shows the MO message flow with RAI = 2, which is similar to that with RAI = 1. Because the RAI value in the NAS PDU is two (in **Step 5.**), the MME should receive DL data from P-GW (in **Step 13.**). After receiving this DL data, the device finishes transmission activities with the network and goes back to RRC_IDLE.

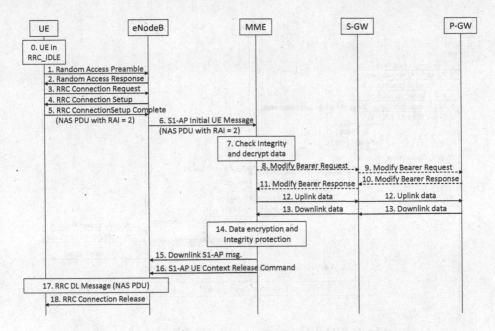

Fig. 2. MO data transport in CP CIoT EPS Optimization with RAI = 2

Note that the device can also transmit data without RAI. In this situation, the basic message flow is the same as that in Fig. 1 (from **Step 0.** to **Step 12.**). After the MME uplinks the data to the P-GW, the connection between the device and the network is not released immediately. The eNB starts the inactivity timer (denoted as T_0). If the device sends or receives data before T_0 expires, the eNB re-starts T_0. Otherwise, the eNB sends the RRC Connection Release command to the device after T_0 expires.

3 Flag-Assisted Early Release of RRC

The operation of the flag-assisted ER-RRC scheme is described in this section. In many IoT applications, the devices sense the environment and report the variation to the remote application server. These devices have MO data much more than MT data. That is when a device uplinks data with RAI = 1, it is far more likely that no pending data is at the MME. Therefore, the eNB can inform the device to enter RRC_IDLE earlier. However, for some cases, the MME might do additional paging if the device releases the RRC connection too early to receive the pending data.

In the flag-assisted ER-RRC scheme, a flag is used to indicate the device has pending data when last time the device enters RRC_IDLE. Additionally, two new IE are added to help the eNB decide whether to release the RRC connection or not. One is called *earlyReleaseRRC* and the other one is called *pendingData*. The modified message flow with ER-RRC is illustrated in Fig. 3. The details are described in the following steps.

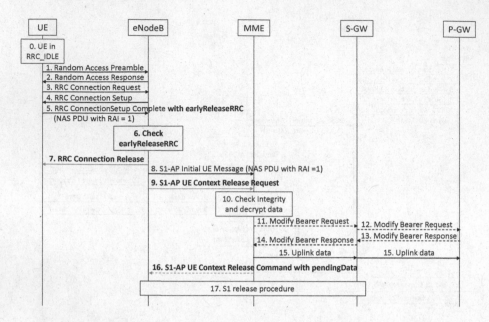

Fig. 3. MO data transport with ER-RRC scheme

Steps 0–4. These steps are the same as that in Fig. 1.

Step 5. In RRC Connection Setup Complete message, *earlyReleaseRRC* is a new IE for the device to set as true, if the device sets RAI value to one.

Step 6. The eNB checks the *earlyReleaseRRC* value before relaying the NAS PDU to the MME.

Step 7. Once the *earlyReleaseRRC* is set to true, the eNB checks the flag. If the flag is false, the eNB immediately releases the RRC connection to the device. The device goes back to RRC_IDLE after receiving this message. In contrast, if the flag is true, the eNB follows CP CIoT message flow instead of ER-RRC.

Steps 8–9. The eNB relays the NAS PDU in S1-AP Initial UE message to the MME. At the same time, the eNB requests the MME to release UE-associated logical S1 connection.

Steps 10–15. The integrity of the data is checked. Before sending the data to P-GW, the MME decrypts the data and requests to re-activate the bearer for the device.

Steps 16–17. The final step is to release the S1 connection between the eNB and the MME. S1-AP UE Context Release Command is one of the messages in S1 release procedure. The *pendingData* is added in S1-AP UE Context Release Command and sent to the eNB. If the MME is aware of pending data, it sets the new IE, *pendingData*, to true.   Once the eNB observes that *pendingData* is true, it sets the flag of the device to true. Otherwise, the eNB sets the flag of the device to false.

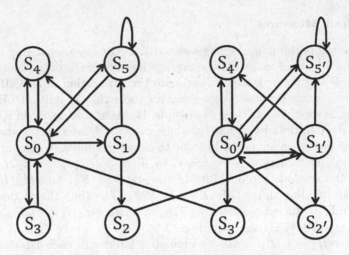

Fig. 4. The Markov chain for the flag-assisted ER-RRC

4   The Analytical Model

An analytical model for flag-assisted ER-RRC by the Markov chain in Fig. 4. UL data arrivals and DL data arrivals are assumed to form a Poisson process with rates λ_u and λ_d, respectively. In other words, the inter-arrival time of UL data, T_u, and the inter-arrival time of DL data, T_d, both follow the exponential distribution with mean $1/\lambda_u$ and $1/\lambda_d$, respectively. The UL data can be classified into three type. Type 1 with the probability α represents the data with RAI = 1 and *earlyRelease*. Type 2 with the probability β represents the data with RAI = 2. Type 3 with the probability γ represents the data without RAI value. Note that $\alpha + \beta + \gamma = 1$. The notations used in the analytical model are shown in Table 1.

In the Markov chain, states, S_i for $i \in [0,5]$, mean the flag is off. If the device transports Type 1 data, the eNB will allow the device to use ER-RRC scheme. In contrast, states, $S_{i'}$ for $i \in [0,5]$, mean the flag is on. The eNB makes the device use CP CIoT. States S_0, $S_{0'}$, S_1, and $S_{1'}$ are RRC_IDLE state. The device in S_0 and $S_{0'}$ has no buffered data at the MME while in S_1 and $S_{1'}$, it does have. The rest states, S_i and $S_{i'}$ for $i \in [2,5]$ are RRC_CONNECTED state where the device wakes up for data transmission. S_2 and $S_{2'}$ denote that the device transmits Type 1 data before the buffered DL data is sent to it. S_3 and $S_{3'}$ denote that the device transmits Type 1 data without buffered data at the MME. S_4 and $S_{4'}$ denote that the device transmits Type 2 data. S_5 and $S_{5'}$ denote that the device transmits Type 3 data or it is paged to receive the buffered data.

4.1   Output Measures

We analyze the performance of flag-assisted ER-RRC by considering the power saving factor (denoted as ω) and the average latency of DL data (denoted as δ). The power saving factor is used to estimate the proportion of RRC_IDLE time in the entire system. Because a device staying more time in RRC_IDLE can save more power, ω should be as large as possible. However, the device in RRC_IDLE cannot receive DL data immediately, which causes DL latency. The target is to enhance the power saving factor but not to cause unaffordable latency.

The whole system time is expressed by $T = \sum_{i=0}^{5} (\pi_i H_i + \pi_{i'} H_{i'})$, where π_i $(\pi_{i'})$ is the stationary probability of the state S_i $(S_{i'})$ and H_i $(H_{i'})$ is the average state holding time of the state S_i $(S_{i'})$. The time that a device stays in RRC_IDLE in the entire system is $T_{idle} = \pi_0 H_0 + \pi_1 H_1 + \pi_{0'} H_{0'} + \pi_{1'} H_{1'}$. Evidently, $\omega = \frac{T_{idle}}{T}$. By the definition, $\delta = \frac{T_{latency}}{N}$, where $T_{latency}$ expressed by $\pi_1 H_1 + \pi_2 H_2 + \pi_{1'} H_{1'}$ is the accumulated latency of each DL data and N expressed by T/λ_d is the number of DL data in the entire system.

4.2   Stationary Probabilities

The transition probability from S_i to S_j $(S_{i'}$ to $S_{j'})$ is denoted as $p_{i,j}$ $(p_{i',j'})$. Take $p_{0,1}$ and $p_{0',1'}$ as an example, the device in S_0 $(S_{0'})$ transits to S_1 $(S_{1'})$ if the DL data arrive earlier than UL data. $p_{0,1}$ and $p_{0',1'}$ can be expressed by $\Pr[T_d < T_u]$. Then, $p_{0,1} = p_{0',1'} = \int_0^\infty \Pr[t_d < t_u | t_u = t] \Pr[t_u = t] dt = \frac{\lambda_d}{\lambda_u + \lambda_d}$. In the same way, we have $p_{0,3} = p_{0',3'} = \alpha \frac{\lambda_u}{\lambda_u \lambda_d}$, $p_{0,4} = p_{0',4'} = \beta \frac{\lambda_u}{\lambda_u \lambda_d}$, $p_{0,5} = p_{0',5'} = \gamma \frac{\lambda_u}{\lambda_u \lambda_d}$, $p_{1,2} = p_{1',2'} = \alpha(1 - e^{-\lambda_u T_{wb}})$, $p_{1,4} = p_{1',4'} = \beta(1 - e^{-\lambda_u T_{wb}})$, $p_{1,5} = p_{1',5'} = \gamma \frac{\lambda_u}{\lambda_u + \lambda_d} + e^{-\lambda_u T_{wb}}$, $p_{5,5} = p_{5',5'} = \frac{\gamma \lambda_u + \lambda_d}{\lambda_u + \lambda_d}(1 - e^{-(\lambda_u + \lambda_d)T_0})$, and $p_{5,0} = p_{5',0'} = \frac{(\alpha+\beta)\lambda_u}{\lambda_u + \lambda_d}(1 - e^{-(\lambda_u + \lambda_d)T_0}) + e^{-(\lambda_u + \lambda_d)T_0}$. Since the device enters $S_{1'}$ when it is in S_2, $p_{2,1'} = 1$. Similarly, $p_{3,0} = p_{4,0} = p_{2',0'} = p_{3',0} = p_{4',0'} = 1$.

By the definition of stationary probability, $\pi_j = \sum_{S_i \in \mathbb{S}} p_{i,j} \pi_i$. If $S_i \in \mathbb{S}$, a device can transit from S_i to S_j directly. Because the stationary probability of each state can be expressed by a function of π_0 and $\sum_{i=0}^{5} (\pi_i + \pi_{i'}) = 1$, all the stationary probabilities can be solved.

4.3   State Holding Time

We assume that the UL or DL data arrive at the jth subframe after the device enters RRC_IDLE (i.e., S_0 and $S_{0'}$) with probability p_j. Then H_0 and $H_{0'}$ can be expressed by $\sum_{j=1}^{\infty} p_j \times j$, where $p_j = \int_{j-1}^{j} f(t, \lambda_u)[1 - F(t, \lambda_d)] dt + \int_{j-1}^{j} f(t, \lambda_d)[1 - F(t, \lambda_u)] dt$, $f(t, \lambda_u)$ $(f(t, \lambda_d))$ is the probability density function (PDF) of the UL (DL) data arrivals, and $F(t, \lambda_u)$ $(F(t, \lambda_d))$ is the cumulative distribution function (CDF) of the UL (DL) data arrivals. p_j can be reformulated as $e^{-(\lambda_u + \lambda_d)(j-1)} - e^{-(\lambda_u + \lambda_d)j}$, $j \in [1, \infty)$. Therefore, $H_0 = H_{0'} = \frac{1}{1 - e^{-(\lambda_u + \lambda_d)}}$.

The DL data arrival time in each eDRX cycle follows an uniform distribution because the time intervals between DL data follow an exponential distribution. On average, the data arrive at the midpoint of an eDRX cycle. That is when a device transits from S_0 to S_1 (or from $S_{0'}$ to $S_{1'}$), it will stay in S_1 ($S_{1'}$) for half of an eDRX cycle on average. Therefore, the average waiting time for the buffered data (denoted as T_{wb}) is $T_{eDRX}/2$, where T_{eDRX} is the length of an eDRX cycle. When a device is at S_1 (or $S_{1'}$), it will leave S_1 ($S_{1'}$) if either the device is paged to receive the buffered data or the device has UL data to transmit before paged. In the latter case, we assume the UL data arrive at the jth subframe after the device enters S_1 (or $S_{1'}$) with probability p_j. $p_j = \Pr[j-1 < T_u < j] = e^{-\lambda_u(j-1)} - e^{-\lambda_u j}, j \in [1, T_{wb}]$. Then, $H_1 = H_{1'} = \Pr[T_u > T_{wb}]T_{wb} + \sum_{j=1}^{T_{wb}} p_j \times j = \frac{1-e^{-\lambda_u T_{wb}}}{1-e^{-\lambda_u}}$.

The time a device spends in S_4 and $S_{4'}$ is three parts: (i) RRC establishment and bearer setup time (including sending the UL data) (denoted as T_{set}); (ii) the latency of the expected DL data (denoted as T_{ed}); (iii) RRC release time (denoted as T_{RR}). More specifically, T_{ed} is the device waiting time for the expected DL data after the device transmits its UL data. We assume T_{ed} follows exponential distribution with mean $1/\lambda_{ed}$. The calculation of part (ii) is the same as H_1 with substituting T_0 for T_{wb}. Thus $H_4 = H_{4'} = T_{set} + \frac{1-e^{-\lambda_{ed} T_0}}{1-e^{-\lambda_{ed}}} + T_{RR}$.

The time a device spends in S_5 and $S_{5'}$ contains T_{set} and four kinds of activities time (T_{RR} included). (1) Type 1 data arrival before T_0 expires. (2) Type 2 data arrival before T_0 expires. (3) Type 3 data or DL data arrival before T_0 expires. (4) no any data arrival. Let $H_5 = H_{5'} = T_{set} + H_{act}$. Note that in $S_{5'}$, since the device is in RRC_CONNECTED, it is supposed to be no buffered data at the MME. Therefore, the eNB informs the device to go back to RRC_IDLE earlier as the device is in case (1). The holding time for (1) is $\sum_{j=1}^{T_0} p_j(j + T_1 + T_{RR})$, where T_1 is the data transmission time. The holding time for (2) is $\sum_{k=1}^{T_0} p_k(k + \frac{1-e^{-\lambda_{ed} T_0}}{1-e^{-\lambda_{ed}}} + T_{RR})$. The holding time for (3) is $\sum_{l=1}^{T_0} p_l(l + H_{act})$. The holding time for (4) is $(\Pr[T_d > T_u > T_0] + \Pr[T_u > T_d > T_0])(T_0 + T_{RR})$. $p_j = \frac{\alpha\lambda_u}{\lambda_u+\lambda_d}(e^{-(\lambda_u+\lambda_d)(j-1)} - e^{-(\lambda_u+\lambda_d)j}), j \in [1, T_0]$. $p_k = \frac{\beta\lambda_u}{\lambda_u+\lambda_d}(e^{-(\lambda_u+\lambda_d)(k-1)} - e^{-(\lambda_u+\lambda_d)k}), k \in [1, T_0]$. $p_l = \frac{\gamma\lambda_u+\lambda_d}{\lambda_u+\lambda_d}(e^{-(\lambda_u+\lambda_d)(l-1)} - e^{-(\lambda_u+\lambda_d)l}), l \in [1, T_0]$. Referring to the reports [17,18], $T_1 = 0.005$ s. Then, we have $H_5 = H_{5'} = \{\frac{1-e^{-(\lambda_u+\lambda_d)T_0}}{1-e^{-(\lambda_u+\lambda_d)}} + e^{-(\lambda_u+\lambda_d)T_0}T_{RR} + \frac{\alpha\lambda_u}{\lambda_u+\lambda_d}(1 - e^{-(\lambda_u+\lambda_d)T_0})(T_1 + T_{RR}) + \frac{\beta\lambda_u}{\lambda_u+\lambda_d}(1 - e^{-(\lambda_u+\lambda_d)T_0})(\frac{1-e^{-\lambda_{ed}T_0}}{1-e^{-\lambda_{ed}}} + T_{RR})\}/\{1 - \frac{\gamma\lambda_u+\lambda_d}{\lambda_u+\lambda_d}(1 - e^{-(\lambda_u+\lambda_d)T_0})\}$.

In states S_2 and S_3, the device wakes up to transmits Type 1 data and goes back to RRC_IDLE. In states $S_{2'}$ and $S_{3'}$, the device has to wait for the MME checking if there are buffered data before going back to RRC_IDLE. Moreover, the device in $S_{2'}$ must spend time to receive the buffered data. Referring to [17,18], $H_2 = H_3 = 0.0335$ s, $H_{2'} = 0.0717$ s, and $H_{3'} = 0.0715$ s.

4.4 Validation

From above deviation, ω and δ can be obtained. The analytical model is validated against discrete event simulation experiments carried out in C++ based simulator. Table 2 shows that the analytical analysis is consistent with the simulation results.

Table 1. Notations used in analytical model

λ_u	UL data arrival rate
λ_d	DL data arrival rate
T	The whole system time
T_u	Inter-arrival time of UL data
T_d	Inter-arrival time of DL data
T_{idle}	Total time a device stays in RRC_IDLE in the entire system
$T_{latency}$	The accumulated latency of each DL data
T_{wb}	The average waiting time for the buffered data
T_{eDRX}	The length of an eDRX cycle
T_{ed}	The latency of the expected DL data.
T_{set}	RRC establishment and bearer setup time (including sending the UL data)
T_{RR}	RRC release time
T_0	The inactivity timer at the eNB
α	The probability of Type 1 UL data
β	The probability of Type 2 data
γ	The probability of Type 3 data
ω	The power saving factor
δ	The average latency of DL data
$\pi_i \ (\pi_{i'})$	The stationary probability of state $S_i \ (S_{i'})$
$H_i \ (H_{i'})$	The average state holding time of state $S_i \ (S_{i'})$
N	The number of DL data in the entire system
$p_{i,j} \ (p_{i',j'})$	The transition probability from S_i to S_j $(S_{i'}$ to $S_{j'})$
$1/\lambda_{ed}$	The mean latency of expected DL data

Table 2. Validation of simulation and analytical models ($T_0 = 10\,\text{s}$, $T_{eDRX} = 10.24\,\text{s}$, and $1/\lambda_{ed} = 5\,\text{s}$).

$1/\lambda_d$	10,000 s			
$1/\lambda_u$	10,000 s		100 s	
RAI setting	$\alpha = \beta = 0$ $\gamma = 1$	$\alpha = 0.4$ $\beta = \gamma = 0.3$	$\alpha = \beta = 0$ $\gamma = 1$	$\alpha = 0.4$ $\beta = \gamma = 0.3$
ω (Ana.)	0.997986	0.99856	0.894281	0.956778
ω (Sim.)	0.997988	0.99856	0.903243	0.957415
Error	0.00%	0.00%	1.00%	0.07%
δ (Ana.)	5.10577	5.10975	4.46125	4.86886
δ (Sim.)	5.10966	5.11149	4.46717	4.86010
Error	0.08%	0.03%	0.13%	0.18%

5 Performance Evaluation

In Fig. 5, the effect of eDRX cycle length on power saving factor and DL latency with three different data arrival rates is observed. Note that the devices set RAI to one for all UL data (i.e., $\alpha = 1$ and $\beta = \gamma = 0$) in this experiment since only RAI value is equal to one, the ER-RRC may be applied. The T_{eDRX} value starts from 10.24 s and the value is doubled each time up to 655.36 s.

Intuitively, when the cycle length becomes large, both power saving factor and DL latency increase. It means that the device spends more time to stay in RRC_IDLE to save more power while the DL data have to wait for longer time to be transmitted to the device. The DL latency is bounded to $1/\lambda_u$ because no matter how large the cycle length is, the DL data can be transmitted when the device has to transport the UL data.

However, it is noticeable that if the arrival rate is too small to consume power, increasing T_{eDRX} cannot well improve ω but makes δ worse. Instead, if the arrival rate is large, setting T_{eDRX} according to the delay budget can greatly enhance ω. Take $1/\lambda = 100$ s for example, if the delay budget is 60 s, T_{eDRX} can be set to 160 s.

Figure 6 shows the effect of the UL arrival rate on ω and δ. We compared flag-assisted ER-RRC scheme with CP CIoT and Always ER which means the eNB makes the device release the connection early every time when the device transmits the Type 1 data. In terms of ω, both flag-assisted ER-RRC and Always ER outperform CP CIoT, because the device in CP CIoT has to wait for the MME checking whether there are buffered data or not, which consumes more power. Although flag-assisted ER-RRC has well performance as Always ER do, δ in flag-assisted ER-RRC is smaller than that in Always ER. The latency is bounded under 5.12 s.

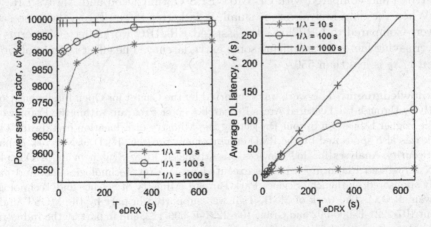

Fig. 5. The effect of eDRX cycle length on ω and δ ($\lambda_u = \lambda_d = \lambda$, $\alpha = 1$, and $T_0 = 1$)

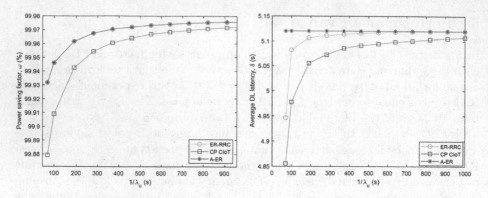

Fig. 6. The effect of UL arrival rate on ω and δ ($\alpha = 1$, $T_0 = 2$ s, $1/\lambda_d = 10{,}000$ s, and $T_{eDRX} = 10.24$ s)

As a final remark, we designed a counter, instead of a flag, in the beginning and defined the threshold to decide whether to fall back to CP CIoT or not. In the experiments, we found that no matter how to set the parameters (i.e., T_0, T_{eDRX}, λ_u, and λ_d), the best outcome is to set the threshold to 1. Based on this result, a complex counter-based ER-RRC is simplified to a flag-assisted ER-RRC.

6   Conclusion

In this paper, the flag-assisted ER-RRC scheme is proposed to help IoT devices save more power. We proposed analytical and simulation models for flag-assisted ER-RRC, and compared with CP CIoT EPS Optimization and Always ER.

When the data arrival rate is small, it is better to set T_{eDRX} large to save power. Compared to CP CIoT, flag-assisted ER-RRC works better in terms of power saving factor by sacrificing some extra latency. The effect is quite obvious when $1/\lambda_u$ is less than 550 s.

Acknowledgment. This work was supported by the Center for Open Intelligent Connectivity through the Featured Areas Research Center Program within the Framework of the Higher Education Sprout Project by the Ministry of Education in Taiwan. This work was also sponsored by the R&D enhancement project "R&D of Network Behavior Security Analyses for IoT Devices on Advanced Edge Switch in an AIOT plus SDN Integrated Platform," which is executed by EstiNet Technologies Inc. and partially sponsored by Hsinchu Science Park Bureau, Ministry of Science and Technology, Taiwan, R.O.C. The work of M.-H. Tsai was supported in part by the MOST under Grant 107-2221-E-006-062 and Grant 108-2221-E-006-112, and in part by the Industrial Technology Research Institute.

References

1. GSA: Global progress to 5G - trials, deployments and launches (July 2018)
2. Cisco: Cisco visual networking index: forecast and trends, 2017–2022 white paper (February 2019)
3. Bujari, A., Furini, M., Mandreoli, F., Martoglia, R., Montangero, M., Ronzani, D.: Standards, security and business models: key challenges for the IoT scenario. Mob. Netw. Appl. **23**(1), 147–154 (2018)
4. 3GPP, TR 45.820 V13.1.0: Cellular system support for ultra low complexity and low throughput Internet of Things (November 2015)
5. 3GPP, TS 24.008 V15.3.0: Mobile radio interface layer 3 specification; Core network protocols; Stage 3 (2018)
6. 3GPP TS 23.401 V14.3.0: General Packet Radio Service (GPRS) enhancements for Evolved Universal Terrestrial Radio Access Network (E-UTRAN) (March 2017)
7. Andres-Maldonado, P., Ameigeiras, P., Prados-Garzon, J., Navarro-Ortiz, J., Lopez-Soler, J.M.: Narrowband IoT data transmission procedures for massive machine-type communications. IEEE Netw. **31**(6), 8–15 (2017)
8. 3GPP: NB-LTE - battery lifetime evaluation (2015)
9. Wang, K., Li, X., Ji, H.: Modeling 3GPP LTE advanced DRX mechanism under multimedia traffic. IEEE Commun. Lett. **18**(7), 1238–1241 (2014)
10. Wang, K., Li, X., Ji, H., Xiaojiang, D.: Modeling and optimizing the LTE discontinuous reception mechanism under self-similar traffic. IEEE Trans. Veh. Technol. **65**(7), 5595–5610 (2016)
11. Chang, H.-L., Tsai, M.-H.: Optimistic DRX for machine-type communications in LTE-A network. IEEE Access **6**, 9887–9897 (2018)
12. Chang, C.-W., Chen, J.-C.: Adjustable extended Discontinuous Reception (eDRX) cycle for idle-state users in LTE-A. IEEE Commun. Lett. **20**(11), 2288–2291 (2016)
13. Lee, J., Lee, J.: Prediction-based energy saving mechanism in 3GPP NB-IoT networks. Sensors **17**(9), 2008 (2017)
14. Xu, S., Liu, Y., Zhang, W.: Grouping-based discontinuous reception for massive narrowband Internet of Things systems. IEEE Internet Things J. **5**, 1561–1571 (2018)
15. 3GPP, TS 24.301 V13.12.0: Non-Access-Stratum (NAS) protocol for Evolved Packet System (EPS) (2018)
16. 3GPP, TS 36.304 V13.8.0: Evolved Universal Terrestrial Radio Access (E-UTRA); User Equipment (UE) procedures in idle mode (2017)
17. 3GPP, TR 25.912 V15.0.0: Feasibility study for evolved Universal Terrestrial Radio Access (UTRA) and Universal Terrestrial Radio Access Network (UTRAN) (2018)
18. Mohan, S., Kapoor, R., Mohanty, B.: Latency in HSPA data networks. Tech. rep., Qualcomm (2011)

DTMFTalk: A DTMF-Based Realization of IoT Remote Control for Smart Elderly Care

Shih-Chun Yuan[1], Shun-Ren Yang[1,2(✉)] ⓘ, I-Fen Yang[1], and Yi-Chun Lin[1]

[1] Department of Computer Science, National Tsing Hua University,
Hsinchu 30010, Taiwan
[2] Institute of Communications Engineering, National Tsing Hua University,
Hsinchu 30010, Taiwan
sryang@cs.nthu.edu.tw

Abstract. Smart elderly care becomes a popular technology to remotely assist the aged at home in recent years because of the population ageing. This paper demonstrates the DTMF-based realization of IoT remote control for telecommunication operators to achieve the smart elderly-care service. By utilizing IoTtalk, we implement a system, DTMFTalk, which supports IoT remote control via conventional circuit-switched DTMF signaling during a phone call conversation. DTMFTalk can monitor the Call State of the smart phone, capture DTMF keys from the in progress call, and send the key values to the IoTtalk server. Afterwards, the smart elderly-care devices can gain the related IoT instructions from the IoTtalk server. Through the delay measurement experiment for DTMFTalk, we observe that DTMFTalk can constantly and accurately recognize the DTMF keys as long as the user holds the desired DTMF keys with enough period.

Keywords: Internet of Things (IoT) · Smart elderly care · Dual Tone Multi-Frequency (DTMF) · Remote control

1 Introduction

In recent years, the smart elderly-care services [2,3,8,9] start developing along with the population ageing. It is becoming more and more common that the aged live alone or family members leave the aged staying at home alone due to working. It is inconvenient for most of the aged to manipulate a lot of essential equipment at home, and danger may even happen in case of carelessness. Thus, the elderly-care service becomes a popular technology to take care of the aged at home. The service can combine some IoT techniques with medical devices, home devices and emergency notification facilities to establish the smart elderly-care service, which can achieve the goal of remotely assisting the aged.

D.-J. Deng et al. (Eds.): SGIoT 2019, LNICST 324, pp. 16–27, 2020.
https://doi.org/10.1007/978-3-030-49610-4_2

Although the smart elderly-care service can integrate with IoT services, there are some existing problems for IoT. The transporting paths of IoT services may involve the public network which cannot guarantee the quality of service (QoS), and various network security problems also exist. Additionally, most of the users install Apps on their smart phones to access IoT services. While the foreground Apps will consume great amounts of power, and the background Apps may cause the users to miss real-time events. Moreover, the cost is very high for managing and maintaining end-to-end Internet-based IoT service platforms with telecom-grade quality. Thus, extra developing the extensive systems is not cost effective for Internet-based IoT service providers.

Circuit-switched telephony network is one of the successful telephony network mechanism in history, and it offers some solutions to existing IoT service problems [6]. For Qos, the transporting paths between the CPEs and the switches are based on the private network, which keeps telecom-grade quality and security. With the telephone number provided by the trust telecommunications operator and routed by their switches, most network security dangers can be blocked. Besides, the CPEs can handle real-time events with lower power consumption like the condition that the users access IoT services deployed on the CPEs through the telephone numbers. Moreover, it is easier and lower cost for telecommunication operators to accommodate IoT services in the existing extensive telecom systems. The related charging mechanisms have been developed for over 100 years and become reliable and flexible, so that IoT services can be charged without extra overhead [7].

In this paper, we propose the approach for telecommunication operators to integrate Dual Tone Multi-Frequency (DTMF) signaling with IoT [5, 10] for Smart Elderly Care. DTMF signaling based on circuit-switched telephony network can also solve some existing IoT problems. DTMF signaling supplies push-button telephones with much higher dialing speed than the dial-pulse signaling used in conventional rotary telephone sets, and it prompts users to select options from menus by sending appropriate DTMF signals from their telephones. Due to the DTMF signaling applications in various fields for years, it becomes one of the familiar technologies for the aged. The smart elderly-care service is provided for the aged, so it is more appropriate for us to choose DTMF signaling to coordinate with the aged habits. Furthermore, we design a system to support IoT remote control via conventional circuit-switched DTMF signaling during a phone call conversation, and we choose to utilize IoTtalk as our IoT service platform.

The following describes the paper organization. Sect. 2 illustrates our system architecture. Sect. 3 further explains how our system captures DTMF signals. Sect. 4 provides the conclusion of our system.

2   The Software Architecture of DTMFTalk

To support IoT remote control via conventional circuit-switched DTMF signaling during a phone call conversation, we design and implement an Android App, DTMFTalk, following the application development/execution framework

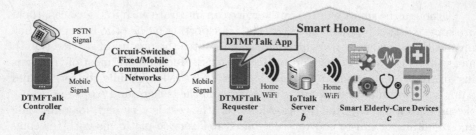

Fig. 1. System architecture

of IoTtalk. Figure 1 illustrates our system architecture, which consists of four components: a DTMFTalk requester a, an IoTtalk server b, several smart elderly-care devices c, and a DTMFTalk controller d. The DTMFTalk requester a is an Android smart phone installed with our DTMFTalk App, while the DTMFTalk controller d is a normal cell or PSTN phone. When the DTMFTalk requester a and the DTMFTalk controller d are in a circuit-switched phone call conversation, the DTMFTalk App is responsible for capturing the DTMF keys embedded inside the audio stream of the call from d, and further transferring the captured DTMF keys to the IoTtalk server b. According to the DTMF keys, the IoTtalk server b continuously manipulates the expected smart elderly-care devices c.

2.1   Overview of the DTMFTalk Software Architecture

The main tasks of DTMFTalk in the DTMFTalk requester a are: (1) to detect if the DTMFTalk controller d (after the authentication and authorization procedures) operates a call conversation with the DTMFTalk requester a, and (2) to capture the DTMF keys from the audio stream and send the keys to the IoTtalk server b. Figure 2 shows the detailed software modules of our DTMFTalk. As illustrated in Fig. 2, DTMFTalk implements two Android application components: the Call Detecting Service (CDS; see Fig. 2(I)) and the DTMF Handling Activity (DHA; see Fig. 2(II)), which handle the above mentioned Tasks 1 and 2, respectively. Note that a typical Android smart phone exercises a state machine for call control in the Android telephony service. Thus, to achieve Task 1, the CDS of DTMFTalk constantly monitors the state machine to retrieve the current call status. The CDS is essentially an Android service, which is responsible for detecting if a call is in progress, and controlling when to perform the DHA. Initially, after DTMFTalk is activated, the CDS is executed in the back end. Whenever a starts to engage in a phone call conversation, the CDS will call to perform the DHA until the phone call conversation is completed. On the other hand, the DHA is an Android activity, which implements the IoTtalk device-side IDA and DA functionalities to capture DTMF keys and send those keys to the IoTtalk server b, respectively. Besides, it provides a user interface for displaying DTMF key related information to the user of a.

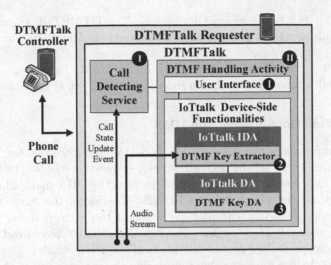

Fig. 2. Software modules of DTMFTalk

2.2   The Functionalities of the CDS

The CDS should, in the back end, continually monitor the call state machine (in particular, its state transitions) in the Android telephony service. The Android telephony call state machine contains three states: the IDLE state, the RINGING state, and the OFFHOOK state. The IDLE state represents that the Android phone has no call activities; the RINGING state represents that a new call arrival occurred and is ringing or waiting; the OFFHOOK state represents that at least one call exists which is dialing, active, or on hold, and no calls are ringing or waiting. By tracking the call state updates, the CDS can be aware if a call is ongoing. We accomplish this via the Android broadcast mechanism. In Android, the system and Apps can send broadcast messages when events of interest, e.g., a call state update in our case, occur. Other Apps can then utilize the Android component `BroadcastReceiver` to register to receive these specific broadcasts. In the implementation, our CDS extends (or inherits) the `BroadcastReceiver` class, in which we specify a receiver that can be notified of a system broadcast message in case a call state update event occurs.

By parsing the received broadcast messages of the call state update events, the CDS can determine the new state after each state update and proceed accordingly. Given the initial state IDLE, a typical state-update sequence and the corresponding reaction of the CDS upon each update are illustrated as follows.

– Update 1 - The new state is RINGING: The DTMFTalk controller invites the DTMFTalk requester, or vice versa, for a call. The CDS can first authenticate and authorize the DTMFTalk controller's telephone number (retrieved via the Caller ID telephone service) before activating the subsequent DTMFTalk tasks.

– Update 2 - The new state is OFFHOOK: The DTMFTalk requester or the DTMFTalk controller accepts the call invitation. The CDS will launch the DHA.

– Update 3 - The new state is IDLE: The DTMFTalk requester or the DTMFTalk controller terminates the call. The CDS will then end the DHA.

2.3 The Functionalities of the DHA

The DHA implements the IoTtalk IDA and DA functionalities for DTMF key capture and delivery to the IoTtalk server, requesting the IoTtalk server to conduct the expected IoT remote control. In fact, the DHA manipulates an IDF *DTMFKey* from the perspective of IoTtalk. Therefore, the main task of the DHA is to update and synchronize the value of the corresponding *DTMFKey* IDF module in the IoTtalk engine. The detailed settings/configurations within the IoTtalk engine for the proper operation of the DHA will be discussed in the later sections. In the following, we summarize the functionalities of the DHA's three components: the *User Interface (UI)*, the *DTMF Key Extractor*, and the *DTMF Key DA*.

– **UI** (Fig. 2(II-1)). The UI is responsible for displaying App views. Besides, the UI also incorporates into the Android component *Text To Speech (TTS)* capability to transform the content of the App views into sounds, assisting the user of the DTMFTalk requester (an elderly person) to use the DTMFTalk App in a more user-friendly manner. Figure 3 shows a snapshot of the UI.

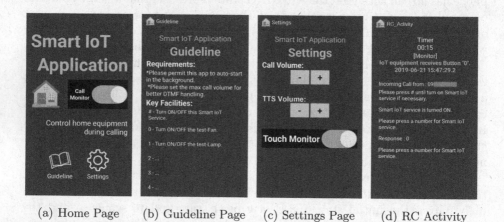

(a) Home Page   (b) Guideline Page   (c) Settings Page   (d) RC Activity Page

Fig. 3. DTMFTalk user interfaces

– **DTMF Key Extractor** (Fig. 2(II-2)). The DTMF Key Extractor uses the Android `AudioRecord` object to access the audio pieces from the audio stream of the ongoing phone call. Afterwards, the DTMF Key Extractor analyzes the audio pieces through the Fast Fourier Transform to determine whether DTMF keys are contained in the call. Moreover, the DTMF Key Extractor can also pass DTMF key related information to the UI, updating the content of the App views. The details of this component will be given in Sect. 3.

- **DTMF Key DA** (Fig. 2(II-3)). The DTMF Key DA is responsible for updating the DTMF key value to the IoTtalk engine. The DTMF Key DA first formulates an HTTP-based RESTful API request by attaching the DTMF key value derived by the DTMF Key Extractor in the message body. Then, the DTMF Key DA delivers the request to the DTMFKey IDF module in the IoTtalk engine to synchronize the IDF value.

3 The Design and Implementation of the DTMF Key Extractor

This section details how we design and implement the DTMF Key Extractor in the DHA of DTMFTalk to capture the DTMF keys from the audio stream of an ongoing phone call. We note that some existing Android Apps, e.g., "DTMF decoder" [4] and "MobIVRS" [12], can already achieve this. These Apps typically perform sound recording first and then conduct decoding analysis on the recorded audio stream. Our DTMF Key Extractor mainly follows the framework of the "MobIVRS" App, which is the most complete open source among the consider Android Apps. However, the "MobIVRS" App, which is actually based on the older Android version, operates with some more inefficient methods and components for most of the current smart phones. Besides, human voices can easily lead the "MobIVRS" App to incorrectly recognize the DTMF keys. In the DTMF Key Extractor, we rearrange the application framework to improve operational efficiency. Moreover, we also introduce and implement the two modes, the *TALKING Mode* and the *DTMF Mode*, in the Main thread to promote the recognition accuracy.

3.1 The Operation of the DTMF Key Extractor

As Fig. 4a illustrates, the DTMF Key Extractor operates a Java-library Blocking Queue (Fig. 4a(1)) and three threads, one for the Main thread (Fig. 4a(2)) and two for the Record Service (Fig. 4a(3)) and the Recognition Service (Fig. 4a(4)), to achieve its tasks. The Blocking Queue is employed to store the *DataBlock* objects, encapsulating the audio pieces recorded by the Record Service, for DTMF key recognition by the Recognition Service. The Blocking Queue has the property that if full, it will block the "producer" (i.e., the Record Service in our case) from putting new objects until the space is released by the "consumer" (i.e., the Recognition Service in our case). In the following, we explain the operation the DTMF Key Extractor in terms of the interactions of its three concurrent threads.

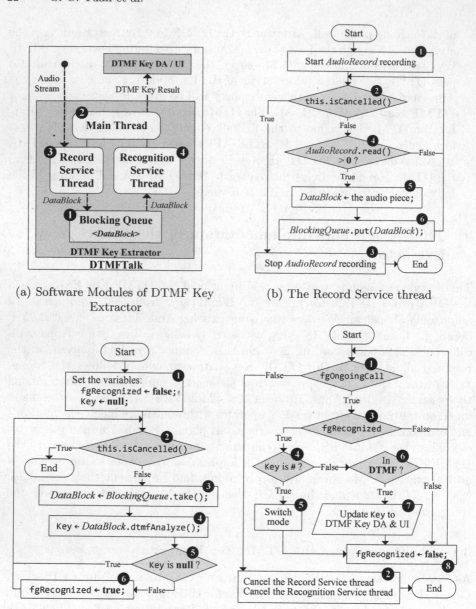

(a) Software Modules of DTMF Key Extractor

(b) The Record Service thread

(c) The Recognition Service thread

(d) The Main thread

Fig. 4. Software modules and operations of the DTMF key extractor

The Record Service Thread. The Record Service thread employs an Android `AudioRecord` object to record the audio stream of the ongoing call. According to the designated audio source, sampling rate, encoding audio format, etc., the `read()` member function of the `AudioRecord` object allows to obtain (from the audio stream) a sampled, quantized, and encoded audio piece in signal format (0 or 1). The Record Service thread then formulates this audio piece as a *DataBlock* object for storing in the Blocking Queue. The operation of the Record Service thread is illustrated in Fig. 4b and is explained as follows. In Step 1, the Record Service thread starts recording by creating an *AudioRecord* object and executing its `startRecording()` method. Next, Steps 2–6 repeatedly read/transform an audio piece and store it in the Blocking Queue until the Record Service thread is terminated by the Main thread. Step 2 first checks whether the thread is cancelled by the Main thread. If **true**, Step 3 will stop recording using the *AudioRecord* object (via the `stop()` method), and then the thread ends; otherwise, Step 4 attempts to read an audio piece from the *AudioRecord* object. In Step 4, if the return value of the `read()` method equals **0**, nothing can be read and the procedure moves back to Step 2 for the next iteration; otherwise, Step 5 transforms the recorded audio piece (stored in a buffer) into a *DataBlock* object, and Step 6 puts the *DataBlock* object into the Blocking Queue.

The Recognition Service Thread. The Recognition Service thread takes and analyzes each *DataBlock* object from the Blocking Queue, checking if any DTMF tone sound is embedded in the audio stream. In case a DTMF tone sound is found, the Recognition Service thread will pass the DTMF key value to the Main thread. Note that the Recognition Service thread uses a Fast Fourier Transform (FFT) to analyze each *DataBlock* object based on the time domain, which will be detailed in the next subsection. The operation of the Recognition Service thread is illustrated in Fig. 4c and is explained as follows. Step 1 initializes the two involved variables, `fgRecognized` (a flag) and Key, as **false** and **null**, respectively. Next, Steps 2–6 repeatedly retrieve and analyze a *DataBlock* object from the Blocking Queue until the Recognition Service thread is terminated by the Main thread. Step 2 first checks whether the thread is cancelled by the Main thread. If **true**, the thread ends; otherwise, Step 3 uses the `take()` method to retrieve a *DataBlock* object from the Blocking Queue. Then, Step 4 analyzes the content of the *DataBlock* object, attempting to derive the embedded DTMF key value and store the result in Key. Step 5 further determines if Key contains a **null** value. If not, a valid DTMF key value is found, and Step 6 will update the shared flag variable `fgRecognized` as **true** to reflect this condition to the Main thread.

The Main Thread. The Main thread controls the operations of the Record Service and Recognition Service threads, and updates valid DTMF key values to the DTMF Key DA and the UI. We note that in a wireless environment, with non-negligible probabilities, normal human audio pieces and even background environment noises can be coincidentally recognized as valid DTMF keys. If the users can first "reveal" when they intend to remotely control (via the DTMF keys) the smart elderly-care devices, the above-mentioned incorrectly identified DTMF keys can be easily ignored, leading to a significantly reduced false DTMF-key detection probability. Besides, in this case, the DTMF Key Extractor can be allowed to only focus on those meaningful DTMF key detections when the users are indeed operating DTMF keys. For this, the Main thread implements two modes: the TALKING mode and the DTMF mode. When the two parties of the call are in conversation, the Main thread stays at the TALKING mode; on the other hand, when the user of the DTMFTalk controller is pressing DTMF keys for remote control, the Main thread stays at the DTMF mode. Moreover, the specific DTMF key '#' is employed to switch between the two modes.

The operation of the Main thread is illustrated in Fig. 4d and is explained as follows. The whole thread repeatedly checks the call status, switches the current mode if necessary, and updates a recognized DTMF key to the DTMF Key DA and the UI until the call is completed. Step 1 first checks the status of the flag, `fgOngoingCall`, which is controlled by the CDS (see Fig. 2(I)), shared with the Main thread of the DTMF Key Extractor, and is used to indicate if the monitored call is still ongoing. If **false**, Step 2 cancels the Record Service and Recognition Service threads, and then the Main thread ends; otherwise, Step 3 checks if the status of the flag, `fgRecognized`, has been set as **true** by the Recognition Service thread, indicating that a DTMF key has been successfully recognized. If a DTMF key has been detected and Step 4 finds that the key is the control key '#', Step 5 switches the mode from **TALKING** to **DTMF**, or from **DTMF** to **TALKING**, depending on the current mode. However, if another DTMF key is found and the current mode is **DTMF** (i.e., the IoT remote control mode) at Step 6, the key can be regarded as a valid key and will be reported to the DTMF Key DA and the UI at Step 7. Finally, before moving back to Step 1 for the next iteration, the `fgRecognized` flag should be reset as **false** at Step 8 to allow the Recognition Service thread to recognize the next DTMF key. Note that for the synchronization among the Main, the Record Service, and the Recognition Service threads, some sophisticated constructs are implemented for the protection of the shared variables. Nevertheless, these details are not presented in this paper due to space limitation.

3.2   The Fast Fourier Transform for DTMF Signal Detection

In Step 4, the Recognition Service thread (see Fig. 4c) performs Fourier analysis for DTMF signal detection [1]. As shown in Fig. 5a, a DTMF signal consists of two tones - with frequencies taken from two mutually exclusive groups: one frequency from the low group (697 Hz, 770 Hz, 852 Hz, 941 Hz), while the other frequency from the high group (1209 Hz, 1336 Hz, 1477 Hz). For example, pressing '3' will generate a 697-Hz tone from the low frequency group along with a 1477-Hz tone from the high frequency group at the same time. Based on such DTMF working principle, the DTMF signal detection in the Recognition Service thread can be achieved as follows.

	1209 Hz	1336 Hz	1477 Hz
697 Hz	1	2	3
770 Hz	4	5	6
852 Hz	7	8	9
941 Hz	*	0	#

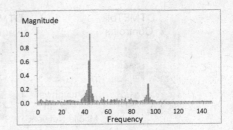

(a) DTMF keypad   (b) The *spectrum* array

Fig. 5. The fast Fourier transform for DTMF signal detection

- When a *DataBlock* object encapsulating the sampled/encoded audio piece for a DTMF signal in the time domain is given, the Cooley-Tukey algorithm [11,13], the most commonly used fast Fourier transform (FFT), is applied to compute the discrete Fourier transform (DFT), a frequency domain representation, of the DTMF signal. This allows to reveal the frequency components that are present in the *DataBlock* object. The output of the Cooley-Tukey FFT algorithm is stored in a **double** array, *spectrum*, of size 150, where the array indices of *spectrum* represent the frequency samples (unit: 15.4 Hz) while the array value of *spectrum* under a given array index represents the corresponding DFT magnitude normalized within [0, 1]. As an example, Fig. 5b illustrates the content of the *spectrum* array after the DTMF signal of '3' is transformed and recorded.
- To determine the corresponding low and high frequencies for the DTMF signal represented by *spectrum*, the Recognition Service thread divides the array indices of *spectrum* into two halves: the low frequencies [0, 74] and the high frequencies [75, 149]. Afterward, the Recognition Service thread searches the frequency with the maximum DFT magnitude in each half, and saves the obtained low frequency in the first half and high frequency in the second half into *lowMax* and *highMax*, respectively. The *lowMax* and *highMax* can be used to look up the corresponding mapping in the DTMF frequency table in Fig. 5a. If matched, the DTMF signal can then be recognized. For example, in Fig. 5b, *lowMax* contains 45 with respect to a frequency value approximately 697 Hz, while *highMax* contains 95 with respect to a frequency value approximately 1477 Hz, which matches the frequency pair of the DTMF signal '3'. Thus, the Recognition Service thread can store the valid key character '3' in *Key*.

3.3   Real Testbed Deployment

We have implemented the functionalities of DTMFTalk, and deployed a real testbed (as shown in Fig. 6) to justify the feasibility of our DTMFTalk as an approach to IoT remote control, especially for elderly-care applications.

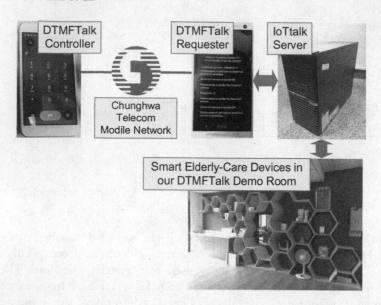

Fig. 6. A real testbed deployment

4   Conclusion

This paper demonstrates how we achieve the integration between DTMF signaling and IoT service. By choosing IoTtalk as the IoT service platform, we design a system called DTMFTalk to support IoT remote control via conventional circuit-switched DTMF signaling during a phone call conversation. DTMF signaling is operated through telephony network, which offers some solutions to existing IoT service problems, such as QoS, network security, power consumption, charging mechanism, maintaining cost and so on. DTMFTalk can monitor the Call State of the smart phone, capture DTMF keys from the in progress call, and send the key values to the IoTtalk server for IoT controlling. Therefore, when DTMFTalk executes in the phone call conversation, the user of the DTMFTalk controller is able to remotely control the smart elderly-care devices by pressing the specific DTMF keys according to the requests coming from the user of the DTMFTalk requester. We perform the delay measurement, which shows that the DTMFTalk controllers can efficiently operate DTMFTalk (within 3 s). Besides, we also explore the background environment noise effect for DTMFTalk. In conclusion, DTMFTalk can constantly and accurately recognize the DTMF keys as long as the user of the DTMFTalk controller holds the desired DTMF keys with enough period.

Acknowledgment. The authors would like to thank Prof. Yi-Bing Lin, CS, NCTU, Taiwan, for his invaluable discussions and suggestions. This work was supported in part by the Ministry of Science and Technology (MOST), Taiwan, under Contracts MOST-108-2221-E-007-034-, MOST-107-2221-E-007-117-MY3, and MOST-106-2923-E-002-005-MY3, in part by the Ministry of Economic Affairs (MOEA), Taiwan, under Contract MOEA-107-EC-17-A-02-S5-007, and in part by the Ministry of Education Higher Education Sprout Project.

References

1. Bhavanam, S.N., Siddaiah, P., Reddy, P.R.: FPGA based efficient DTMF detection using split goertzel algorithm with optimized resource sharing approach. In: 2014 Eleventh International Conference on Wireless and Optical Communications Networks (WOCN), pp. 1–8, September 2014. https://doi.org/10.1109/WOCN.2014.6923072
2. Borelli, E., et al.: Habitat: an IoT solution for independent elderly. Sensors **19**(5), 1258 (2019). https://doi.org/10.3390/s19051258
3. Ghasemi, F., Rezaee, A., Rahmani, A.M.: Structural and behavioral reference model for IoT-based elderly health-care systems in smart home. Int. J. Commun. Syst. **32**(12), e4002 (2019). https://doi.org/10.1002/dac.4002. https://onlinelibrary.wiley.com/doi/abs/10.1002/dac.4002
4. Jasiun, P.: DTMF decoder (2011). https://github.com/pjasiun/dtmf-decoder
5. Johar, R.A., Fakieh, E., Allagani, R., Qaisar, S.M.: A smart home appliances control system based on digital electronics and GSM network. In: 2018 15th Learning and Technology Conference (L&T), pp. 52–58, February 2018. https://doi.org/10.1109/LT.2018.8368485
6. Lin, Y., Lin, R., Chen, Y., Twu, C., Yang, S.: Deploying the first PSTN-based IoT mechanism. IEEE Wirel. Commun. **25**(6), 4–7 (2018). https://doi.org/10.1109/MWC.2018.8600748
7. Lin, Y.B., Sou, S.I.: Charging for Mobile All-IP Telecommunications. Wiley, Chichester (2008)
8. Liu, Y., et al.: A novel cloud-based framework for the elderly healthcare services using digital twin. IEEE Access **7**, 49088–49101 (2019). https://doi.org/10.1109/ACCESS.2019.2909828
9. Lu, Y., Lin, C.: The study of smart elderly care system. In: 2018 Eighth International Conference on Information Science and Technology (ICIST), pp. 483–486, June 2018. https://doi.org/10.1109/ICIST.2018.8426110
10. Noman, A.T., Rashid, H., Chowdhury, M.A.M., Islam, M.S.: Design implementation of a microcontroller based low cost DTMF controlled acoustic visual detecting robot to monitor child aged person. In: 2019 International Conference on Electrical, Computer and Communication Engineering (ECCE), pp. 1–6, February 2019. https://doi.org/10.1109/ECACE.2019.8679401
11. Sedgewick, R., Wayne, K.: Algorithms, 4th edn. Addison-Wesley Professional, Reading (2011)
12. Sharma, N., Jain, R., Garg, M., Arya, S.: Mobivrs (2015). https://github.com/SharmaNishant/MobIVRS
13. Sorensen, H., Heideman, M., Burrus, C.: On computing the split-radix FFT. IEEE Trans. Acoust. Speech Signal Process. **34**(1), 152–156 (1986). https://doi.org/10.1109/TASSP.1986.1164804

IoT Insider Attack - Survey

Morshed U. Chowdhury[1]([⊠]), Robin Doss[1], Biplob Ray[2], Sutharshan Rajasegarar[1], and Sujan Chowdhury[2]

[1] Center for Cyber Security Research and Innovation (CSRI), Deakin University, Geelong, Australia
{morshed.chowdhury,robin.doss,
suthershan.rajasegarar}@deakin.edu.au
[2] Centre for Intelligent Systems (CIS), Central Queensland University, Rockhampton, Australia
{b.ray,s.chowdhury2}@cqu.edu.au

Abstract. The "Internet of things" (IoT) creating a perfect storm in the smart world. Due to the availability of internet and capabilities of devices, sensors-based technologies becoming popular day by day. It now opens the opportunities for overcoming many new challenges. Any device with on/off capability connecting through the internet via sensor can be an IoT device which includes a coffee machine, light, hand watch, headphones, washing machine, mobile phones, car, CCTV camera and so on. Simply we can say connecting things to people via the internet and controlling remotely is the great advantage of IoT. In our daily life, the IoT is widely used which includes transportation, health, education, security and so on. Imagine how IoT can make our life easier, based on your set alarm when you wake up if it can notify your coffee machine to prepare coffee for you that will save you time. Despite those advantages, the IoT based system is not free from vulnerabilities. Different types of attacks make the system vulnerable and tried to exploit the system and creating obstacles from its growth. Here we will explore IoT attacks and the relevant technologies associated along with machine learning strategies that exist to overcome those obstacles.

Keywords: IoT · Insider attack · Mitigation technique · IoT application · Machine learning

1 Introduction

The Internet of Things (IoT) can act in three different ways, firstly, collecting information and sending it to the appropriate location, secondly, acting on collected information in an intelligent way and finally doing both automatically. For example, sensors like temperature, weather, light, moisture, air quality sensors can automatically collect information from the environment and make more intelligent decisions like watering land and send information when crops need to be cut. The applications of IoT have grown exponentially in a short period of time over the utility industry as well. Now a day's smart grids for electricity, water and gas dominated by IoT. These varieties of use cases enhanced customer service and at the same time increase the overall value of a business. Beyond

© ICST Institute for Computer Sciences, Social Informatics and Telecommunications Engineering 2020
Published by Springer Nature Switzerland AG 2020. All Rights Reserved
D.-J. Deng et al. (Eds.): SGIoT 2019, LNICST 324, pp. 28–41, 2020.
https://doi.org/10.1007/978-3-030-49610-4_3

this, we can apply IoT technology for smart health initiatives by monitoring heart rate of an individual and alert nearby hospital or relatives in case of any emergency. It can be applicable in automobile industry to check the tire pressure using sensors and alert the driver if the tire pressure goes below limit. Thus, IoT adding value to the business and change the way of business operations. Investors need to change the ways of their business for the benefits of their organizations.

The main goal of IoT can be expressed as the following ways:

- Improve overall business experience
- Save money and time
- Improve the productivity of the employees
- Help investors for taking quick decisions
- Improve customer experience
- Generate more profit
- Keep the business model up to date with modern technologies

Because of the benefits of IoT technologies, it expands in numerous sectors like industry, individual and government which cover all areas of our life. Nowadays individual can control their home appliances like heating, lighting and electronic devices via smartphones and other internet accessible devices.

Not only controlling home but also wearing smartwatch as well as other wearable sensors is the most common fashion among the people with different ages. Those wearable sensors can collect and analyze data and give useful feedback on individual health which makes life easier and more comfortable. In case of emergency with the help of other sensors can respond quickly to provide an optimized route by tracking construction works or any other emergency work on the route. The IoT makes a significant contributions in health sector which includes real time health monitoring for patients and give instant results by analyzing and predicting possible problems. Sensors also can be used for inventory management and order automatically if stock reached a specific threshold.

Because of on growing growth of human being crises on electricity is one of the biggest issues all over the world. Using the advancement of sensors in IoT systems, the temperature can be adjusted by counting the number of people in the building as well as in the room. Automatically shutting down the lights and air conditioner if there are no occupants and control the temperature accordingly also one of the biggest achievements in the area of IoT. Not only in our daily life but also in the agriculture sector lots of improvement has been done and some are ongoing. Smart farming can monitor temperature, soil moisture, predicting rain, humidity level to do the watering and fertilizing the land. Sensors can predict the time of irrigating and can automatically pick up the selected crops from the land. The same technique can be applied to control the streetlight in a smart city. Sensors also can be used to monitor environmental concerns in terms of heavy traffic.

As illustrated in Fig. 1, the IoT is the center of our evolving smart world where automation, connectivity and productivity are not confined within a specific silo. The connectivity between objects, individual and computing devices from diverse silos are working together for smarter future in every steps of our life.

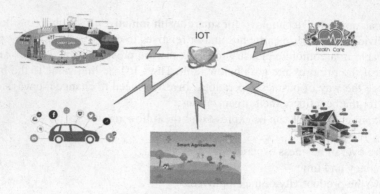

Fig. 1. IOT application scenario

Beyond the above-mentioned advantages, security and privacy is a great concern in IoT. As billions of sensors connect over the internet to collect and support the technologies it involves billions of data point which need to be secured to avoid data manipulation. As many people will try to take advantage by manipulating the data and make the system vulnerable for their own benefit, therefore, IoT security is one of the important focus research areas in the smart world.

The 2016 Dyn cyberattack is one of the biggest DDoS attack in IoT which makes most of the DNS (domain name server) vulnerable. This impact a large number of internet accessible devices which includes printer, baby monitor, security cameras and so on. The attack is known as Mirai botnet attack which is a malicious program which can replicate itself by exploiting poorly secured IoT devices and gain access by a central server. A manufacturer who didn't update their IoT product periodically became insecure hence prone to attacks.

As sensors are holding personal information like name, ages, mobile number, addresses even social network account therefore hackers can compromise these sensors and sale to relevant agencies. Not only hackers but also other risk factors like natural disasters, electricity, infrastructure also needs to be considered to make the overall system secure.

This paper will focus on the IoT attacks and what are the security mechanism taken so far to stop those known attacks. This research will also try to highlight the gaps and possible areas of improvement within the existing techniques.

2 Survey on IoT Attacks

In this section, we will discuss attacks based on layers architecture of IoT presented in Fig. 2. It is very important to understand the attack layers and types of attacks happen in each layer then it will be helpful to identify the causes. As illustrated in Fig. 2, we have presented the IoT network in four main layers where perception and sensing layers are accommodating most of the revolving IoT technologies. For example, Routing Protocol for Low-Power and Lossy Networks (RPL), RFID (Radio Frequency Identification) and WSN (Wireless Sensor Networks) are the technologies used by IoT which belong to the last two layers as mentioned previously.

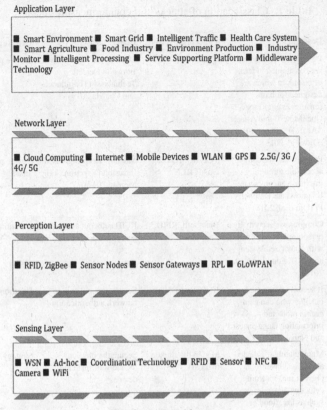

Fig. 2. IoT architecture

In next sub-section, we have presented attacks taxonomy based on our detail analysis of exiting literature.

2.1 IoT Attack Taxonomy

The attack happens at different levels based on the weakness and depends on the techniques of the security attacks. We start by categorizing of different IoT attacks and countermeasures in Table 1 which also presented the link of different protocols with the categories. As we can see in Table 1, the IoT attacks can be classified based on targeted technologies, nature of intrusion as well as penetration vicinity like from inside or outside. It might be a hardware or software attack. But most of the time it is software-based attack and there is also a possibility of physical or natural disaster-based attack.

In Fig. 3, we have presented the IoT attack taxonomy based on the existing attacks reported in the literature and in Table 1. The Fig. 3 presents a clearer IoT taxonomy which demonstrated that existing IoT attacks explored various IoT technologies by inside and outside intruders who are targeting to compromise mainly three areas: information, operation and access level of devices.

Table 1. Classification of attacks and countermeasures detail

Attacks	Description	Protocols involved	Countermeasures	Category
Low end class	Low power device that are constrained in terms of resources which are designed for basic sensing. Examples are OpenMote-B and Atmel SAMR21 Xplained-Pro (Ojo et al. 2018)	UART, SPI, I2C	Deep-Learning-Driven Intrusion Detection Techniques (Thamilarasu and Chawla 2019)	Device property-based attack
High end class	Powerful device can be accessible through internet from anywhere. Examples are Raspberry Pi (Ojo et al. 2018)	TCP-IP, MQTT, CoAP, BLE	Machine Learning based Intrusion Detection (Yair Meidan 2017)	Device property-based attack
Insider attack	Compromise security by a person or by code itself with authorized system access (Kammüller et al. 2016)	Bluetooth, RFID, Zeebee	RFID authentication and encryption techniques	Location based attack
Outsider attack	If security comprise by outsider who can gain access protected information (Jang-Jaccard and Nepal 2014)	IP, TCP or DNS	Secure channel and do network authentication	Location based attack
Physical	Manipulating the device at physical layer to prevent sensors from detecting general risks such as fire, flood or unexpected motion (Ali and Awad 2018)	Man in the middle (MITM)	Secure the physical locations of installed devices	Strategy
Logical	Communication channel interrupted by external attack without damaging physical device (Ali and Awad 2018)	COAP, XAMP, HTTP	Security protocols based on AES	Strategy
Passive	When an attacker doesn't manipulate any information but can read all the traffic is known as passive attack. Attackers always looking for open ports and vulnerabilities of a system (Arış et al. 2018)	RPL	Automata Based Intrusion Detection Method	Access level
Active	When an attacker cause damage or manipulate information when gain access is known as active attack. (Nurse et al. 2015)	RPL	Network-Based Detection of IoT Botnet Attacks Using Deep Autoencoders (Meidan et al. 2018)	Access Level

(*continued*)

Table 1. (*continued*)

Attacks	Description	Protocols involved	Countermeasures	Category
Disruption	When availability of IOT device interrupted by attackers then it known as protocol disruption	RPL	Classification based detection (Zhang et al. 2014)	Protocol Based
Deviation	When attacker writes malicious code on the IOT system is known as deviation from the protocol. Examples like DDOS attack (Mustapha and Alghamdi 2018)	Application and Network Protocol	Rule based detection	Protocol Based
Interception	Also known as man in the middle attack where the attacker secretly read all the message and intercept the message	MTTM	SWAP: Mitigating XSS Attacks using a Reverse Proxy (Wurzinger et al. 2009)	Information Damage Level
Fabrication	By fabricating information in IOT device attacker damage the normal architecture of the system. Example like blackhole attack	RPL	Mitigation of black hole attack (Ahmed and Ko 2016)	Information Damage Level
Interruption	When a fake message is inserted into the IOT network by an intruder and gain control is known as interruption. Examples of this attack like unwanted shut down of IOT device	Network protocol	Software-Defined Internet of Things Framework (Yin et al. 2018)	Information Damage Level
Eavesdropping	Eavesdropping occurs when attacker will be able to install traffic monitoring system within the IOT device	Network protocol	A hybrid prevention method for eavesdropping attack by link spoofing (Tri-Hai Nguyen, 2017)	Information Damage Level
User	If a authenticate user explode security credential, make the device accessible	N/A	Logging user activities	Host Based
Hardware	Hardware tempering is another way of attack IOT device	N/A	Securing the hardware	Host Based
Software	Software within the IOT device if not updated periodically and if there is bug in the software can create damage in the overall IOT system	N/A	Updating the software	Host Based

(*continued*)

Table 1. (*continued*)

Attacks	Description	Protocols involved	Countermeasures	Category
Link	By doing repetitive collision and transmitting same frequency to the IOT devices simultaneously can create the attack	RPL	Link-layer metric as a parameter in the selection of the default route (Wallgren et al. 2013a)	Communication Stack Protocol (CSP)
Network	By creating loop in the routing table or by duplicating the node in the network creates the attack	RPL		CSP
Transport	Like DDOS and hello flood attack	RPL		CSP
Application	Sending malicious or fishing attack	RPL		CSP

ZigBee is a popular wireless communication technology for sensor communication. To get a further understanding of IoT device-based attacks, in Table 2, we have illustrated attacks under device based technologies. As we can see from Table 2, although there are a large number of existing attacks based on Wi-Fi communication technology, the ZigBee based attacks are on the rise due to its popularity in sensor communication.

2.2 IoT Routing Attacks

To further explore routing attacks in IoT, this article has presented existing attacks in RPL (Routing Protocol for Low-Power and Lossy Networks) based IoT networks in Table 3. The RPL is a popular routing protocol for sensor networks in IoT. As presented in Table 3, attacks are ground in three main categories based on their objectives. In the resource category, the attacks aim to compromise network resources using direct and indirect techniques which ultimately cause DoS attack. The topology of the sensor networks is dynamic which exploited by many attacks listed in the topology category. Finally, the attacks in traffic category eavesdrop sensors traffic over the insecure wireless network to identify vulnerabilities. As RPL works with low power and lossy network, it is difficult to find a full proof adaptive countermeasure as presented in the countermeasure section of Table 3 which shows most of the existing countermeasures are attack detection techniques.

2.3 RFID Attacks

RFID is an integral part of IoT technology like sensory tags due to its unique identification capability over the wireless medium. RFID tags are two types – active and passive and attack happens in both types. Despite the advantage of RFID readers security of the device gets compromised due to the limitation of RFID hardware. There are many attacks exist in RFID network which could be an easy entry point to the IoT network. In Fig. 4,

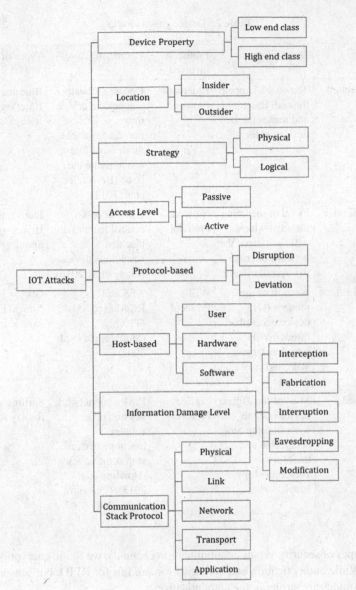

Fig. 3. IoT attack taxonomy

we have presented the taxonomy of existing RFID attacks which are categorized based layers of IoT network detailed in Fig. 1.

There are many lightweight techniques proposed by researchers in RFID tags and in readers to counter these RFID attacks detailed in Fig. 4. For example, lightweight sanitization technique (Ray et al. 2011 and Xiao et al. 2016), authentication techniques (Ahemd et al. 2017) and stenography (Ray et al. 2013) are some examples. As mentioned earlier, the virus can spread through RFID tags (Li et al. 2012) to the IoT networks. If we

Table 2. Device based attacks

Attacks	Descriptions	Protocols involved	Countermeasures	Types of attacks
Bluetooth Based Attack	The attack happens through Bluetooth and makes the IOT devices vulnerable	Bluetooth Protocol	Update software and put the device into non-discoverable mode or offline can mitigate the issue (Be-Nazir et al. 2012)	Bluesnarfing, BlueBugging, Bluejacking
Denial of Service	Flood of incoming message which will slow down the network or crush the overall system	Network Protocol	Using access control list and do blacklist suspicious devices (Liang et al. 2016)	Interception, Hijacking, Spoofing
Wifi Based Attack	As most of the modern IOT device accessible through WiFi intruders target WiFi and create damage	WEP Protocol	AES and RC4-based SSL (TLS) (Stubblefield et al. 2002)	Google Replay Attack, FMS Attack and so on
ZigBee based Attack	Most of the Zigbee device operate without using any encryption and therefore vulnerable for attack	ZigBee Protocol	Pre install network key and do a counter mechanism can stop some attack (Dowling et al. 2017), (Olawumi et al. 2014)	Sniffing and Replay Attack

compare types of security versus communication channels, we found encryption is weak in RFID. While authentication and authorization are fair for RFID, but sensor gateway and sensor nodes are strong in the authentication.

3   IoT Attacks and Future Research

Uses of IoT devices is increasing day by day. Recent research shows 20 billion IoT devices up-and-running so far. The number will be enormously increase as the 5G mobile network will dominate within few years which will connect more and more IoT devices. This large pool of internet connected devices will increase our dependency on the IoT network which will bring new vulnerabilities in light. The Mirai Botnet attack (Abdur Razzaq et al. 2017) might cause more damage and make it easy for bad guys to cause

Table 3. RPL Attack

Attack		Descriptions	Protocols involved	Countermeasures	Types of attacks
Resources	Direct Attack	Attackers directly exhaust the resources	RPL, User Datagram Protocol (UDP), Constrained Application Protocol (CoAP)	Intrusion detection mechanism with a lightweight heartbeat protocol (Wallgren et al. 2013a)	Flooding, Routing table overload
	Indirect Attack	Attacks happened from another malicious node	RPL, User Datagram Protocol (UDP), Constrained Application Protocol (CoAP)	Data path validation mechanism (Mangelkar et al. 2017), RPL loop detection and avoidance mechanisms (Kamble et al. 2017)	Increase rank attack, DAG inconsistency, Version attack
Topology	Sub optimization	Manipulate the routing table	TinyAODV Protocol, MintRoute Protocol	SVELTE (Raza et al. 2013), Rank verification, Parent fail-over, Geographical data, Merkel trees	Routing table falsification, Sinkhole, Wormhole, RI play, Worst parent
	Isolation	Isolating node from the actual communication in the network	AODV Protocol	Monitoring of counters	Blackhole, DAO Inconsistency
Traffic	Eavesdropping	Doing eavesdropping activities by deploying attacker node	HTTP, TELNET, FTP, POP, SNMP	Encryption	Traffic analysis, Sniffing
	Misappropriation	Discovering the topology of the network through malicious activity	Demand Source Routing (DSR), Optimized Link State Routing (OLSR), Zonal Routing Protocol (ZRP)	VeRA (Dvir et al. 2011), TRAIL (Landsmann et al. 2013)	Decreased rank attack, Identity attack

global damage. Now, most people use wearable devices which could be potentially affected by IoT attacks. The automated DevOps testing device from a less professional vendor might create security risk (Zhou et al. 2019). Furthermore, the shadow IT resource and IT professionals within the organization might be a serious concern for IoT networks.

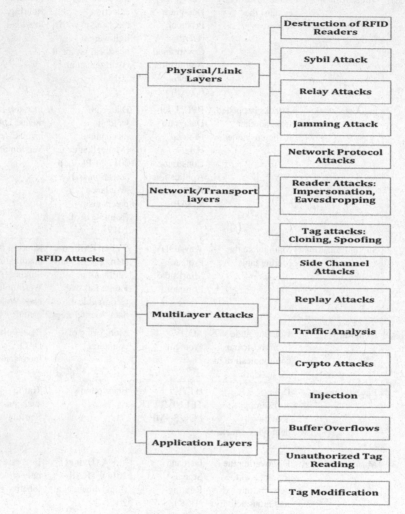

Fig. 4. RFID Attacks

Outdated hardware might be the biggest security challenge and automated identification of these weak devices will be one of the future research challenges. Although the growth of big data is not a big problem yet but as time pass by bigdata will be a serious concern due to gowning difficulties of the management and analysis of the dataset. Due to so much personal data collected by big companies via IoT, the security breaches will create a great damage for consumers. So, securing those personal data and create a technique of automatically destroying those data will be a future research direction for IoT security. The adaptive security techniques will be more effective to protect IoT network, therefore, a great deal of future research on IoT security will find an appropriate adaptive security that can learn from the live network and implement countermeasure thereafter.

4 Conclusion

IoT will be the future. Despite some security challenges, the IoT will dominate in every place which will cover from home to industry. This paper tries to highlight all the current attacks and known security issues which is already mitigated by different techniques. If the security mechanism is not taken properly those attacks can still cause great harm in the IoT network. Despite these known attacks, there will be unknown attacks and new security breach which need to be taken into consideration, hence adaptive security measures will be our future to protect IoT network.

References

Abdur Razzaq, M., Habib, S., Ali, M., Ullah, S.: Security issues in the Internet of Things (IoT): a comprehensive study. Int. J. Adv. Comput. Sci. Appl. (IJACSA) 8(6), 383–388 (2017)

Ahemd, M.M., Shah, M.A., Wahid, A.: IoT security: a layered approach for attacks & defenses. Paper presented at the 2017 International Conference on Communication Technologies (ComTech), 19–21 April 2017

Ahmed, F., Ko, Y.B.: Mitigation of black hole attacks in routing protocol for low power and lossy networks. Secur. Commun. Netw. 9(18), 5143–5154 (2016)

Ali, B., Awad, A.: Cyber and physical security vulnerability assessment for IoT-based smart homes. Sensors 18(3), 817 (2018)

Arış, A., Oktuğ, S.F., Voigt, T.: Security of Internet of Things for a reliable Internet of Services. In: Ganchev, I., van der Mei, R.D., van den Berg, H. (eds.) Autonomous Control for a Reliable Internet of Services. LNCS, vol. 10768, pp. 337–370. Springer, Cham (2018). https://doi.org/10.1007/978-3-319-90415-3_13

Be-Nazir, N., Ibn Minar, N., Tarique, M.: Bluetooth security threats and solutions: a survey. Int. J. Distrib. Parallel Syst. 3(1), 127 (2012)

Dowling, S., Schukat, M., Melvin, H.: A ZigBee honeypot to assess IoT cyberattack behaviour. Paper Presented at the 2017 28th Irish Signals and Systems Conference (ISSC), 20–21 June 2017

Dvir, A., Holczer, T., Buttyan, L.: VeRA - version number and rank authentication in RPL. Paper Presented at the 2011 IEEE Eighth International Conference on Mobile Ad-Hoc and Sensor Systems, 17–22 October 2011

Jang-Jaccard, J., Nepal, S.: A survey of emerging threats in cybersecurity. J. Comput. Syst. Sci. 80(5), 973–993 (2014)

Kamble, A., Malemath, V.S., Patil, D.: Security attacks and secure routing protocols in RPL-based Internet of Things: survey. Paper Presented at the 2017 International Conference on Emerging Trends & Innovation in ICT (ICEI), 3–5 February 2017

Kammüller, F., Nurse, J.R.C., Probst, C.W.: Attack tree analysis for insider threats on the IoT USING Isabelle. In: Tryfonas, T. (ed.) HAS 2016. LNCS, vol. 9750, pp. 234–246. Springer, Cham (2016). https://doi.org/10.1007/978-3-319-39381-0_21

Landsmann, M., Wahlisch, M., Schmidt, T.C.: Topology authentication in RPL. Paper Presented at the 2013 IEEE Conference on Computer Communications Workshops (INFOCOM WKSHPS), 14–19 April 2013

Li, H., Chen, Y., He, Z.: The Survey of RFID attacks and defenses. Paper Presented at the 2012 8th International Conference on Wireless Communications, Networking and Mobile Computing, 21–23 September 2012

Liang, L., Zheng, K., Sheng, Q., Huang, X.: A denial of service attack method for an IoT system. Paper Presented at the 2016 8th International Conference on Information Technology in Medicine and Education (ITME), 23–25 December 2016

Mangelkar, S., Dhage, S.N., Nimkar, A.V.: A comparative study on RPL attacks and security solutions. Paper Presented at the 2017 International Conference on Intelligent Computing and Control (I2C2), 23–24 June 2017

Meidan, Y., et al.: N-BaIoT—network-based detection of IoT botnet attacks using deep autoencoders. IEEE Pervasive Comput. **17**(3), 12–22 (2018). https://doi.org/10.1109/MPRV.2018.033 67731

Mitrokotsa, A., Rieback, M.R., Tanenbaum, A.S.: Classifying RFID attacks and defenses. Inf. Syst. Front. **12**(5), 491–505 (2010). https://doi.org/10.1007/s10796-009-9210-z

Mustapha, H., Alghamdi, A.M.: DDoS attacks on the Internet of Things and their prevention methods. Paper Presented at the Proceedings of the 2nd International Conference on Future Networks and Distributed Systems, Amman, Jordan (2018)

Nawir, M., Amir, A., Yaakob, N., Lynn, O.B.: Internet of Things (IoT): taxonomy of security attacks. Paper Presented at the 2016 3rd International Conference on Electronic Design (ICED), 11–12 August 2016

Nurse, J.R.C., Erola, A., Agrafiotis, I., Goldsmith, M., Creese, S.: Smart insiders: exploring the threat from insiders using the Internet-of-Things. Paper Presented at the 2015 International Workshop on Secure Internet of Things (SIoT), 21–25 September 2015

Ojo, M., Giordano, S., Procissi, G., Seitanidis, I.: A review of low-end, middle-end and high-end IoT devices. IEEE Access **6**, 70528–70554 (2018)

Olawumi, O., Haataja, K., Asikainen, M., Vidgren, N., Toivanen, P.: Three practical attacks against ZigBee security: attack scenario definitions, practical experiments, countermeasures, and lessons learned. Paper Presented at the 2014 14th International Conference on Hybrid Intelligent Systems, 14–16 December 2014

Raza, S., Wallgren, L., Voigt, T.: SVELTE: real-time intrusion detection in the Internet of Things. Ad Hoc Netw. **11**(8), 2661–2674 (2013). https://doi.org/10.1016/j.adhoc.2013.04.014

Stubblefield, A., Ioannidis, J., D. Rubin, A.: Using the Fluhrer, Mantin, and Shamir Attack to break WEP (2002)

Thamilarasu, G., Chawla, S.: Towards deep-learning-driven intrusion detection for the Internet of Things. Sensors **19**(9), 1977 (2019). https://doi.org/10.3390/s19091977

Tri-Hai Nguyen, M.Y.: A hybrid prevention method for eavesdropping attack by link spoofing in software-defined Internet of Things controllers. Int. J. Distrib. Sens. Netw. (2017)

Wallgren, L., Raza, S., Voigt, T.: Routing attacks and countermeasures in the RPL-based Internet of Things. Int. J. Distrib. Sens. Netw. **9**(8), 794326 (2013a). https://doi.org/10.1155/2013/794326

Wurzinger, P., Platzer, C., Ludl, C., Kirda, E., Kruegel, C.: SWAP: mitigating XSS attacks using a reverse proxy (2009)

Yair Meidan, M.B., Shabtai, A., Ochoa, M., Tippenhauer, N.O., Guarnizo, J.D., Elovici, Y.: Detection of unauthorized IoT devices using machine learning techniques (2017). https://arxiv.org/abs/1709.04647

Yin, D., Zhang, L., Yang, K.: A DDoS attack detection and mitigation with software-defined Internet of Things framework. IEEE Access **6**, 24694–24705 (2018). https://doi.org/10.1109/ACCESS.2018.2831284

Zhang, K., Liang, X., Lu, R., Shen, X.: Sybil attacks and their defenses in the Internet of Things. IEEE IoT J. **1**(5), 372–383 (2014). https://doi.org/10.1109/JIOT.2014.2344013

Zhou, W., Jia, Y., Peng, A., Zhang, Y., Liu, P.: The effect of IoT new features on security and privacy: new threats, existing solutions, and challenges yet to be solved. IEEE IoT J. **6**(2), 1606–1616 (2019)

Ray, B., Huda, S., Chowdhury, M.U.: Smart RFID reader protocol for malware detection. In: 2011 12th ACIS International Conference on Software Engineering, Artificial Intelligence, Networking and Parallel/Distributed Computing, Sydney, NSW, 2011, pp. 64–69 (2011)

Ray, B.R., Chowdhury, M., Abawajy, J.: StenoCipher to provide data confidentiality and tampered data recovery for RFID tag. In: Lee, R. (ed.) Software Engineering, Artificial Intelligence, Networking and Parallel/Distributed Computing 2012. Studies in Computational Intelligence, vol. 443, pp. 37–51. Springer, Berlin (2012). https://doi.org/10.1007/978-3-642-32172-6_4

Ray, B., Chowdhury, M., Abawajy, J.: Hybrid approach to ensure data confidentiality and tampered data recovery for RFID tag. Int. J. Netw. Distrib. Comput. **1**(2), 79–88 (2013)

Energy Management for Zones-Based Isolated DC Multi-microgrids

Arshad Nawaz[1], Jing Wu[1(✉)], Chengnian Long[1], and Yi Bing Lin[2]

[1] Department of Automation, School of Electronic Information and Electrical Engineering, Key Laboratory of System Control and Information Processing, Ministry of China, Shanghai Jiao Tong University, Shanghai, China
jingwu@sjtu.edu.cn
[2] Department of Computer Science and Information Engineering, National Chiao Tung University, Hsinchu 300, Taiwan
liny@cs.nctu.edu.tw

Abstract. In this paper, zones based distributed energy management for isolated multi-microgrids is proposed. Loads are categorized into different zones to form zonal multi-microgrids. Each microgrid has own energy management system which can locally manages the supply and demand of its zonal load and minimize the operational cost. Distributed Network Operator (DNO) act as central controller to facilitate the energy exchange between zonal microgrids and balancing the overall system-wide supply and demand in economic way. Demand Response Program (DRP) is also utilized for peak load shifting within the scheduling horizon. In addition to minimization of operation cost, the utilization of DR will also assure the reliability of supply. In the proposed distributed energy management, each microgrid balances its supply and demand locally and exchange surplus and deficit power with other microgrids through DNO. The performance of proposed scheme is demonstrated through case study simulation of radial multi-microgrid structure.

Keywords: Energy management · Isolated multi-microgrids · Load zones

1 Introduction

Microgrid (MG) is combination of loads, Energy Storage Systems (ESSs), DGs and interfacing converters with an energy management system (EMS) to regulate the power generation and its consumption. MGs have two modes of operation: a) Grid-Connected Mode, b) Islanded Mode. MG tends to maximize the benefit of microgrid in grid-connected mode while in islanded mode of operation, its objective is to improve the reliability and security in emergency events [1, 20, 24]. The uncertainties in renewable power generation, market prices of electricity, and penetration of electrical vehicles (EVs) and time varying load demand pose challenges for optimal operation of MG [13, 16, 21, 23]. Several MGs can be combined together to form a multi-microgrids (MMG) in order to substantially handle

D.-J. Deng et al. (Eds.): SGIoT 2019, LNICST 324, pp. 42–56, 2020.
https://doi.org/10.1007/978-3-030-49610-4_4

the uncertainties [25]. In the recent past, a lot of research has been carried out relating to architecture and configuration of MMG system. The primary goals of MMG system are to minimize the operation cost, system wide supply reliability, balance of supply/demand for each individual microgrid [8].

The EMS architecture for MMG could be centralized, decentralized or hybrid depending on the objective under consideration. In centralized EMSs, the energy balance of entire network is managed by central EMS. However, with expansion of network size, the computational stress on central EMS also increases promptly [11,12,17]. Furthermore, centralized control is vulnerable to single point of failure and lacks plug & play capabilities [6]. The centralized controller requires reconfiguration with addition of new load or generator to the system. Additionally, the central EMS requires scheme of energy generation and utilization of each microgrid, therefore creating privacy concerns and also require an intensive communication infrastructure [2,7,19].

The decentralized EMS, in contrast to centralized EMS, has local EMS for individual microgrid. Local EMS of microgrid can communicate with other local EMS in network through communication infrastructure. The amount of information transfer is less compared to centralized scheme and therefore consequently there is less computational burden [9,14,18].

In an MMG system, each MG and the distribution network operator (DNO) can participate as independent units. However, with a coordinated EMS, both the DNO and MG owners could decrease their operational costs and the costumers could profit from a more reliable and secure electrical power [3]. Demand response programs (DRPs) are also utilized in MMG structures for more reliable supply in recent past [3,15]. Load curve of MG can be reshaped and peak loads can be reduced and transferred in time to other off-peak time slot through utilization of DRP schemes. In [10] a distributed energy management with price elasticity based DR scheme is proposed for interconnected operations of MGs. The time of use (ToU) based DR program is utilized in energy management for distribution system and multi-microgrids cooperative network in [5]. The energy management is formulated as multi follower bi-level game problem and is solved from DNO prospective to maximize profit. A bi-level model is proposed in [22] for economic operation of distributed network and microgrids. The control variable considered for upper level are the grid power and electricity price of MGs and the lower level variables are power of DG and the DN. In order to investigate the effect of demand response on residential load in the proposed work, real time pricing DRP is considered.

The majority of existing work is focused on the energy management of multi-microgrids in grid connected mode. The energy management of multi-microgrids operating in isolated mode still need further research and attention. The supply is always less then demand in grid isolated mode of multi-microgrid operation and therefore the objective of individual microgrid in isolated mode is different from the case of grid-connected mode of operation. This paper proposes distributed energy management of zonal load based multi-microgrid in isolated mode with consideration of demand response program. The similar set of loads are divided into zones are prioritized on bases of load type. Demand response program is utilized to reduced cost and increase the reliability of individual MG.

The rest of the paper is organized as follows. Section 2 presents the system description and modeling. Section 3 explains the proposed strategy for energy management of multi-microgrid arrangement operating in grid isolated mode and objective functions are presented. In Sect. 4 case study simulation are provided to show effectiveness of proposed model. Finally, conclusion is document in Sect. 5.

2   System Description and Modeling

2.1   Zonal Multi-microgrids

In this section, a new concept of zonal microgrid is explained. In previous conducted research work, the microgrid is composed of composite community loads (hospital, school and residential). The load curve, due to composite loads, is very fluctuating and it is challenging task to maintain the supply and demand balanced. By separately categorizing identical loads into specific sets of load and forming a specific category load zones can achieve defined load curve and the supply and demand could be easily achieved.

In this proposed work, the various type of community loads (hospital, school and residential) are categorized into zones of identical load type to form zonal microgrid. Each microgrid represent one zone. The zone formations with identical load sets help in obtaining defined load curve for day-ahead scheduling of energy resources in particular microgrid. The small scale energy zones or zonal MGs operates in grid-isolated mode. These zonal microgrids can exchange surplus/deficit energy with each other through Distributed Network Operator (DNO). There is no direct exchange of power between microgrids. Each zonal microgrid has its own local Energy management for managing its energy resources in order to keep supply and demand balance locally.

The propose zonal microgrids general structure is illustrated in Fig. 1. Each zone has one type of load (Residential, Hospital or School). The considered distributed generation resources in each zone are photo-voltaic (PV) panel, wind turbine (WT) and diesel generator (DG). The detail mathematical models of sources, energy storage system and load are discussed in proceeding sections.

2.2   Load Model

The load of each zone is categorized in three type, I) Critical loads, II) deferrable loads and III) Interruptible loads. The user demand of i_{th} zone is represented by $P_{L_m}^t$ and is mathematically given as:

$$P_{L_m}^t = P_{CL_m}^t + \Delta P_{L_m}^t + P_{in_m}^t \tag{1}$$

here the subscript m represent the zonal microgrid and is defined as $m \in Z_i$, where $Z_i = \{Z_1, Z_2, ..Z_n\}$. Whereas $P_{L_m}^t$, $P_{CL_m}^t$, $\Delta P_{L_m}^t$ and $P_{in_m}^t$ are the forecasted load Demand, Critical Load, Defferable Load and Interruptable Load of

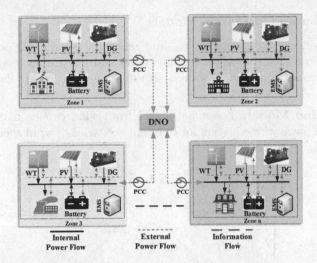

Fig. 1. General representation of Zonal Multi-microgrids structure

the zoned microgrid at time t and are subject to following constraints.

$$P_{L_m}^{min} \leq P_{L_m}^t \leq P_{L_m}^{max} \qquad \forall t \in \mathcal{T}, \forall m \in Z_i \qquad (2)$$

$$\Delta P_{L_m}^{min} \leq \Delta P_{L_m}^t \leq \Delta P_{L_m}^{max} \qquad \forall t \in \mathcal{T}, \forall m \in Z_i, \qquad (3)$$

$$P_{in_m}^{min} \leq P_{in_m}^t \leq P_{in_m}^{max} \qquad \forall t \in \mathcal{T}, \forall m \in Z_i \qquad (4)$$

The constraints (2)–(4) shows the maximum and minimum limits of total zone load, deferrable and interruptible loads.

2.3   Energy Storage Modeling

The energy storage play important role in balancing supply and demand of islanded microgrids. The energy could be stored during off peak hours or in case of availability of surplus energy in microgrid. Likewise, the stored energy can e provided to balance the demand in case of peak hours or shortage of energy. Battery is considered as energy storage source in this paper and its operating constraints are given as:

$$U_{ch}^t P_{B,ch_m}^{min} \leq P_{B,ch_m}^t \leq U_{ch}^t P_{B,ch_m}^{max}, \qquad \forall t \in \mathcal{T}, \forall m \in Z_i \qquad (5)$$

$$U_{dis}^t P_{B,dis_m}^{min} \leq P_{B,dis_m}^t \leq U_{dis}^t P_{B,dis_m}^{max}, \qquad \forall t \in \mathcal{T}, \forall m \in Z_i \qquad (6)$$

$$U_{ch,dis}^t \in \{0,1\} \qquad \forall t \in \mathcal{T}, \forall m \in Z_i \qquad (7)$$

$$U_{ch}^t + U_{dis}^t \leq 1 \qquad (8)$$

$$SoC_{B_m}^t = SoC_{B_m}^{t-1} + (\eta_B^{ch} P_{B,ch_m}^t - P_{B,dis_m}^t / \eta_B^{dis}) \Delta t \qquad (9)$$

$$SoC_{B_m}^{min} \leq SoC_{B_m}^t \leq SoC_{B_m}^{max} \qquad \forall t \in \mathcal{T}, \forall m \in Z_i \qquad (10)$$

here P_{B,ch_m}^t, P_{B,dis_m}^t, $SoC_{B_m}^t$ represent charging, discharging and state of charge of the battery respectively.

2.4   Distributed Generation Models

We have considered both conventional and renewable sources for power generation in microgrid. Renewable sources like wind and PV are not being dispatchable and where as conventional sources like diesel generators are dispatchable.

Wind Turbine Model. Power harnessed from wind can be mathematically modeled with piece-wise equation for different scenarios of wind speed. It can be written in mathematical form as [4]:

$$P_{WT_m}^t = \begin{cases} 0 & 0 \le v^t \le v_{ci} \\ P_r \times \dfrac{v^t - v_{ci}}{v_r - v_{ci}} & v_{ci} \le v^t \le v_r \\ P_r & v_r \le v^t \le v_{co} \\ 0 & v_{co} \le v^t \end{cases} \qquad \forall t \in \mathcal{T}, \forall m \in Z_i \qquad (11)$$

where $P_{WT_m}^t$ is power generated by wind turbine of Zone$_i$ at time t, v^t is expected wind speed, v_{ci} is cut in speed, v_r is rated speed and v_{co} is cut off speed.

PV Model. The output power os PV is greatly depended on the solar irradiance (W/m^2) and ambient temperature (°C). The power generated by solar PV can be expressed as:

$$P_{PV_m}^t = P_s \frac{G_{Irr}}{G_s} [1 + k (T_c - T_r)] \qquad \forall t \in \mathcal{T}, \forall m \in Z_i \qquad (12)$$

Where G_{Irr}, G_s and k are the solar incident irradiance, maximum irradiance at standard test $(1000 \, \text{W/m}^2)$ and temperature coefficient respectively. coefficient of PV power generation. The T_c, T_r and P_s represents PV cell temperature, reference temperature and maximum power at standard test respectively.

Generator Model. A conventional DG unit such as diesel is a dispatch-able source, its output power is a variable with the following constraints:

$$P_{G_m}^{min} \times U_m^t \le P_{G_m}(t) \le P_{G_m}^{max} \times U_m^t, \qquad \forall t \in \mathcal{T}, \forall m \in Z_i$$

$$U_m^t \in \{0,1\} \qquad \forall t \in \mathcal{T}, \forall m \in Z_i \qquad (13)$$

$$ramp_{G_m}^{down} \Delta t \le [P_{G_m}(t) - P_{G_m}(t-1)] \le ramp_{G_m}^{up} \Delta t,$$

$$\forall t \in \mathcal{T}, \forall m \in Z_i \qquad (14)$$

Constraint (13) illustrates the maximum and minimum permissible limit for the generated power of the particular DG. Constraint (14) emphasize on the ramp up and ramp down limitation of each DG. The cost function of a diesel generator follows a quadratic function of its generated power and can be expressed as follows:

$$Cost P_{G_m}^t = \alpha (P_{G_m}^t)^2 + \beta (P_{G_m}^t) + \gamma \qquad (15)$$

Furthermore, a start up cost has been taken into account for the avoidance of frequent starting up or shutting down of diesel generator as below:

$$Cost_{up} = U_m^t \times st_{cost}^{Up} \tag{16}$$

here U_m^t shows the commitment status of the generator, its value can either be 1 for commitment state and 0 for non-commitment state. Consequently, the integrated cost of the diesel generator can be written as:

$$Cost_{G_m}^t = CostP_{G_m}^t + Cost_{up} \tag{17}$$

2.5   Demand Response Program

Demand Response Program (DRP) objective is to change user load demand according to variation in system power. The microgrid has the capability to shift its load from peak hours to off-peak hours with utilization of DRP and reduce cost of energy supply. DRP has various possible ways of employing such as load shifting, load curtailment and so on. We have utilized load shifting scheme and suppose that specific amount of load (20% of total load) can participate in DRP. The system load after applying DRP can be written in mathematical from as follow [5].

$$P_{LDR_m}^t = (1 - DR^t).P_{L_m}^t + ldr^t \qquad \forall t \in \mathcal{T}, \forall m \in Z_i, \tag{18}$$

$$DR^t \le DR^{max} \qquad \forall t \in \mathcal{T}, \forall m \in Z_i, \tag{19}$$

$$\sum_{t-1:T} ldr^t = \sum_{t-1:T} (DR^t) \times (P_{L_m}^t) \qquad \forall t \in \mathcal{T}, \forall m \in Z_i \tag{20}$$

here $P_{LDR_m}^t$, ldr^t, and $P_{L_m}^t$ represents the percentage of load shifting from hour t, Shifted load from other hours t to hour t', and forecasted power demand at time t of MG, respectively.

The constraint in Eq. 19 limits the load portion that is to be shifted to off-peak time. Equation 20 shows the total assignable load and assure that daily consumption of energy will remain the same after utilization of DRP.

3   Proposed Scheme

The EMS for zonal MGs is explained and objective functions of MGs and DNO have been formulated in this section. In the proposed zonal multi-microgrid structure, MGs and DNO have their own objective functions. The problem of energy management has been solved in two steps in order to complete one round of optimization. At the first step, EMS of each MG receives the hourly information of its load profile and generation capacities as input and local optimization is performed with consideration of demand response program. EMS schedules its DERs locally to balance the supply/demand and computes deficit and surplus power as shown in Algorithm 1. The DNO is informed about surplus/deficit power status with request to sale/buy power to/with other zone's microgrid. DNO receives the information of surplus/deficit power from each zone and prioritize zones according to load priority. Global optimization is performed to balance system-wide supply and demand in second step using Algorithm 2.

The DNO has to deals with two cases. Case 1) supply/demand deficit, Case 2) Supply/demand surplus. In case of deficit power, DNO sales power to the zone with high priority first. The sensitive load zone microgrid supply and demand is balanced first and then other zones are served accordingly. Likewise, in case of surplus power, extra power is traded with other zonal microgrid while considering the priority of zones. This concludes first round of optimization.

In order to facilitate exchange of power among microgrids and achieve over all supply-demand balance, the following policy is considered by the DNO.

1. The load demand of high priority zone microgrid will be supplied at high priority all of the time.
2. In case of power deficiency in high priority zone microgrid, DNO will sale it power first.
3. The load demand of other zones will be meet next and DNO will consider sale of power to other zones after serving high priority zone first.

Algorithm 1. Local EMS

1: Get values of load and generation forecast;
2: Run local optimization for each microgrid
3: **for** $t < T$ **do**
4:   **if** $P_m^t = P_{LDR_m}^t$ **then**
5:     No deficit and surplus power
6:   **else if** $P_m^t < P_{LDR_m}^t$ **then**
7:     Calculate deficit power
8:     Check battery charge status
9:     **if** $SoC \geq 80\%$ **then**
10:       Discharge battery
11:     **else if** $SoC \leq 20\%$ **then**
12:       Send request to DNO for buying power
13:     **end if**
14:   **else if** $P_m^t > P_{LDR_m}^t$ **then**
15:     Calculate surplus power
16:     Send request to DNO for selling power
17:   **end if**
18:   t++
19: **end for**

3.1   Microgrids Objective Function

The objective of each microgrid in proposed model is to balance its supply and demand with minimal operational cost. The objective function of individual microgrid provided in Eq. (21) contains CDG generation cost, startup cost for CDG, power trading cost, and battery charging and discharging cost at time t interval of scheduling horizon. The scheduling horizon considered in this paper is 24 h with interval of one hour.

$$\min \sum_{t \in T} Cost^t_{G_m} + \sum_{t \in T} (\lambda_{buy} \times P^t_{def_m} - \lambda_{sale} \times P^t_{sur_m})$$
$$+ \sum_{t \in T} Cost^t_{B_m} (P^t_{B_m,dis} - P^t_{B_m,ch}) \tag{21}$$

$$s.t :$$

$$\sum_{t \in T} (P^t_{PV} + P^t_{WT} + P^t_{DG} + P^t_{B_m,dis} + P^t_{def_m})$$
$$= \sum_{t \in T} (P^t_{LDR_m} + P^t_{B_m,ch} + P^t_{sur_m}) \qquad \forall t \in T, \forall m \in Z_i$$

$$\tag{22}$$

and constraint (2)–(10), (13)–(14) and (18)–(20).

Here λ_{buy}, λ_{sale}, $P^t_{def_m}$ and $P^t_{sur_m}$ represents the buying price, selling price, deficit power and surplus power respectively. Eqs. (2)–(4) provides the upper and lower bounds for individual MG load. The operating limits and start-up cost of generator is also considered and given by constraints (13)–(14). Power generated by microgrid DG should balance the load demand at each interval and is given by (22). The maximum amount of shift-able load is constrained by (19). The load after applying DR (load shifting) can be computed by using Eq. (18). Each MG computes its surplus and shortage power amount according to Algorithm 1 and after the execution of local optimization by each MG-EMS, theses values are conveyed to the DNO.

3.2   DNO Objective Function

The DNO receives the information of surplus and deficit powers from each microgrid and performs global optimization in second step. The objective of DNO is to guarantee over all system-wide balance of supply and demand in economic way. In order to formulate objective function for DNO, the cost of buying (selling) from (to) is required to be considered. The objective function for DNO is given

---

Algorithm 2. Energy exchange

1: Initial values;
2: Gets power status of each microgrid
3: Prioritize microgrid
4: **for** $t < T$ **do**
5:    **for all** $i < N$ **do**
6:       **if** Deficit power$t > 0$ **then**
7:          sale power to high priority MG first
8:       **end if**
9:       **if** Surplus power> 0 **then**
10:          Buy surplus power from MG
11:          **if** supply& demand balanced **then**
12:             Go to step 18
13:          **else**
14:             Charge battery
15:          **end if**
16:       **end if**
17:    **end for**
18:    t++
19: **end for**

---

by Eq. (23) and it contains cost of buying power from MG and cost of selling power to MG.

$$\min \sum_{m \in Z_i} \sum_{t \in \mathcal{T}} (\lambda_{buy}^t \times P_{buy_m}^t - \lambda_{sale}^t \times P_{sale_m}^t) \tag{23}$$

Subject to:

$$\sum_{t \in \mathcal{T}} \sum_{m \in MG} (P_{PV_m}^t + P_{WT_m}^t + P_{DG_m}^t + P_{B_m,dis}^t + P_{buy_m}^t)$$

$$= \sum_{t \in \mathcal{T}} \sum_{m \in MG} (P_{LDR_m}^t + P_{B_m,ch}^t + P_{sale_m}) \qquad \forall t \in \mathcal{T}, \forall m \in Z_i \tag{24}$$

$$\sum_{t \in \mathcal{T}} \sum_{m \in MG} P_{def_m}^t = \sum_{t \in \mathcal{T}} \sum_{m \in MG} P_{sur_m}^t \qquad \forall t \in \mathcal{T}, \forall m \in Z_i \tag{25}$$

$$P_{sur_m}^{min} \leq P_{sur_m}^t \leq P_{sur_m}^{max}, \qquad \forall t \in \mathcal{T}, \forall m \in Z_i \tag{26}$$

$$P_{def_m}^{min} \leq P_{def_m}^t \leq P_{def_m}^{max}, \qquad \forall t \in \mathcal{T}, \forall m \in Z_i \tag{27}$$

The energy exchange between microgrids and DNO is performed according to Algorithm 2. The constraint (24) guarantee the system wide balance of supply and demand, where is the balance of deficit and surplus power is constrained by (25).

4   Case Study Simulation

In this section a case study is considered to illustrate the effectiveness of proposed algorithm. The configuration is shown in Fig. 2. Three interconnected microgrids

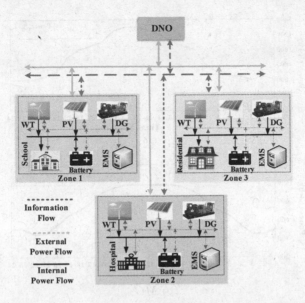

Fig. 2. Considered case study for multi-microgrids energy management

are operated in grid-isolated mode. Each microgrid represents a categorized load zone. The zones are prioritized according to load sensitivity. The hospital load zone has higher priority then school load. The least priority is given to residential load zone. The microgrids can exchange energy through DNO. The DNO does not contain any generating unit and load point. Each microgrid consists of conventional generator (diesel), Wind turbine and PV source. The parameters of diesel generators for each microgrid are listed in Table 1. The proposed energy management is performed in two steps and operation of each step explained in proceeding subsection for case study simulation.

Table 1. Cost coefficients of microgrids diesel generator

Parameter	MG_1	MG_2	MG_3
Capacity (kW)	300	200	200
α (¥/kWh^2)	0.0056	0.0061	0.0061
β (¥/kWh)	0.142	0.091	0.091
γ (¥)	0.221	0.184	0.184
Start-up cost (¥)	0.9	0.7	0.7

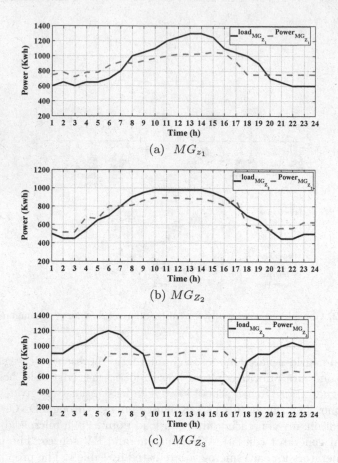

Fig. 3. Power and Load demand forecast of (a) MG_{Z_1} (b) MG_{Z_2} (c) MG_{Z_3}

4.1 Step 1

The local EMS of individual microgrid gets the information of its load forecast and available generation for energy management in scheduling horizon. The scheduling horizon considered in this work is 24 h with interval of one hour each. The load and generation forecast for each microgrid is shown in Fig. 3. It can be clearly seen that in isolated mode, the generated power, in three MGs, is less then required load demand. It can be observed from Fig. 3(a) that, the peak load interval of MG_{Z_1} is from 8am to 18pm. Likewise, from Fig. 3(b), the peak load interval of MG_{Z_2} is from 8am to 16pm.

Whereas, peak load interval of MG_{Z_3} is between 1am to 8am and 18pm to 24pm as shown in Fig. 3(c). The load from these intervals will be shifted to the off-peak intervals after applying DR in step 1. The local EMS of each microgrid apply DRP to the initial forecasted load demand and solve the local optimization problem to schedules its generating units accordingly. The Surplus

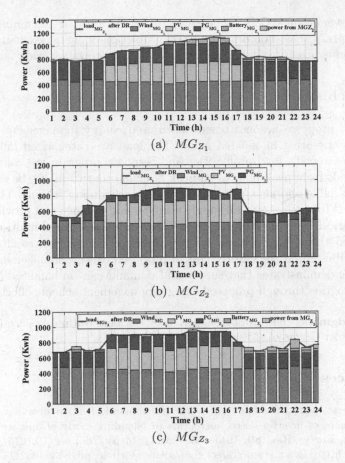

Fig. 4. Energy schedule of (a) MG_{Z_1} (b) MG_{Z_2} (c) MG_{Z_3}

and deficit power is calculated as a difference of supply and demand. The status of individual surplus and deficit power is communicated to DNO for possible sale and purchase of energy in either case.

4.2   Step 2

In second step, DNO receives the power status of each microgrid and prioritize each microgrid according to load. Hospital zone has high priority than school and school priority is higher than residential. The DNO perform as central controller in order to facilitate prioritize energy exchange between MGs and guarantee system wide supply and demand balance. The DNO make decision based upon the received energy status of corresponding MG. In this case study, MG_{Z_1} and MG_{Z_3} has deficit power. The DNO gives preference to MG_{Z_1} due to its high priority. The surplus power in MG_{Z_2} is first sold to MG_{Z_1} to balance its power deficiency. The remaining power is sold to MG_{Z_3}. This is shown in Fig. 4(a), surplus power from MG_{Z_2} is first soled to MG_{Z_1} and the remaining power is offered to MG_{Z_3} based on priority. After completion of energy exchange, if there is still surplus power available, it is utilized for charging batteries.

5   Conclusion

This paper proposes a zones based distributed energy management for multi-microgrids operating in isolated mode. The load are categorized into different zones to get specific load profile. Demand response program are considered for shifting loads from peak hour to off peak hour in order to make the energy supply more reliable and also facilitate the energy scheduling scheme. The focus of this paper is to achieve over all supply and demand balance and provide reliable power to prioritized critical load zones. The reliability of zonal multi-microgrids is enhanced through prioritized energy exchange. Simulation results are performed to illustrated the effectiveness of proposed energy management scheme. The results demonstrates that supply and demand can be balanced in isolated multi-microgrids through proposed energy management scheme effectively.

Acknowledgment. This work is supported by National Natural Science Foundation of China under Grants 61873166, 61673275 and 61473184.

References

1. Andishgar, M.H., Gholipour, E., llah Hooshmand, R.: An overview of control approaches of inverter-based microgrids in Islanding mode of operation. Renew. Sustain. Energy Rev. **80**, 1043–1060 (2017). https://doi.org/10.1016/j.rser.2017.05.267. http://www.sciencedirect.com/science/article/pii/S1364032117309140
2. Xia-Dou, C., Gian-Wang, W., Hao, D.W., Bin-Li, X.: Mas-based solution to energy management strategy of distributed generation system. Int. J. Electr. Power Energy Syst. **69**, 354–366 (2015). https://doi.org/10.1016/j.ijepes.2015.01.026. http://www.sciencedirect.com/science/article/pii/S0142061515000563
3. Haider, H.T., See, O.H., Elmenreich, W.: A review of residential demandresponse of smart grid. Renew. Sustain. Energy Rev. **59**, 166–178 (2016). https://doi.org/10.1016/j.rser.2016.01.016. http://www.sciencedirect.com/science/article/pii/S1364032116000447
4. Hammerstrom, D.J.: Ac versus dc distribution systems did we get it right? In: 2007 IEEE Power Engineering Society General Meeting, pp. 1–5, June 2007. https://doi.org/10.1109/PES.2007.386130
5. Jalali, M., Zare, K., Seyedi, H.: Strategic decision-making of distribution network operator with multi-microgrids considering demand response program. Energy **141**, 1059–1071 (2017)
6. Jun, Z., Junfeng, L., Jie, W., Ngan, H.: A multi-agent solution to energymanagement in hybrid renewable energy generation system. Renew. Energy **36**(5), 1352–1363 (2011). https://doi.org/10.1016/j.renene.2010.11.032. http://www.sciencedirect.com/science/article/pii/S0960148110005458

7. Karavas, C.S., Kyriakarakos, G., Arvanitis, K.G., Papadakis, G.: A multi-agentdecentralized energy management system based on distributed intelligence forthe design and control of autonomous polygeneration microgrids. Energy Conv. Manag. **103**, 166–179 (2015). https://doi.org/10.1016/j.enconman.2015.06.021. http://www.sciencedirect.com/science/article/pii/S0196890415005610
8. Kou, P., Liang, D., Gao, L.: Distributed EMPC of multiple microgrids for coordinated stochastic energy management. Appl. Energy **185**, 939–952 (2017). https://doi.org/10.1016/j.apenergy.2016.09.092. http://www.sciencedirect.com/science/article/pii/S0306261916313964
9. Lee, J., Guo, J., Choi, J.K., Zukerman, M.: Distributed energy trading in microgrids: a game-theoretic model and its equilibrium analysis. IEEE Trans. Industr. Electron. **62**(6), 3524–3533 (2015). https://doi.org/10.1109/TIE.2014.2387340
10. Liu, N., Wang, J., Wang, L.: Distributed energy management for interconnectedoperation of combined heat and power-based microgrids with demand response. J. Mod. Power Syst. Clean Energy **5**(3), 478–488 (2017). https://doi.org/10.1007/s40565-017-0267-2. https://doi.org/10.1007/s40565-017-0267-2
11. Nikmehr, N., Najafi Ravadanegh, S.: Optimal power dispatch of multi-microgrids at future smart distribution grids. IEEE Trans. Smart Grid **6**(4), 1648–1657 (2015). https://doi.org/10.1109/TSG.2015.2396992
12. Nikmehr, N., Ravadanegh, S.N.: Reliability evaluation of multi-microgrid sconsidering optimal operation of small scale energy zones underload-generation uncertainties. Int. J. Electr. Power Energy Syst. **78**, 80–87 (2016). https://doi.org/10.1016/j.ijepes.2015.11.094. http://www.sciencedirect.com/science/article/pii/S0142061515005256
13. Nisar, A., Thomas, M.S.: Comprehensive control for microgrid autonomous operation with demand response. IEEE Trans. Smart Grid **8**(5), 2081–2089 (2017). https://doi.org/10.1109/TSG.2016.2514483
14. Parisio, A., Wiezorek, C., Kyntäjä, T., Elo, J., Strunz, K., Johansson, K.H.: Cooperative MPC-based energy management for networked microgrids. IEEE Trans. Smart Grid **8**(6), 3066–3074 (2017). https://doi.org/10.1109/TSG.2017.2726941
15. Paterakis, N.G., Erdinç, O., Catalão, J.P.: An overview of demand response: keyelements and international experience. Renew. Sustain. Energy Rev. **69**, 871–891 (2017). https://doi.org/10.1016/j.rser.2016.11.167. http://www.sciencedirect.com/science/article/pii/S1364032116308966
16. Rabiee, A., Sadeghi, M., Aghaeic, J., Heidari, A.: Optimal operation of microgrids through simultaneous scheduling of electrical vehicles and responsive loads considering wind and pv units uncertainties. Renew. Sustain. Energy Rev. **57**, 721–739 (2016). https://doi.org/10.1016/j.rser.2015.12.041. http://www.sciencedirect.com/science/article/pii/S1364032115014240
17. Vaccaro, A., Loia, V., Formato, G., Wall, P., Terzija, V.: A self-organizing architecture for decentralized smart microgrids synchronization, control, and monitoring. IEEE Trans. Industr. Inf. **11**(1), 289–298 (2015). https://doi.org/10.1109/TII.2014.2342876
18. Wang, Y., Mao, S., Nelms, R.M.: On hierarchical power scheduling for the macrogrid and cooperative microgrids. IEEE Trans. Industr. Inf. **11**(6), 1574–1584 (2015). https://doi.org/10.1109/TII.2015.2417496
19. Wang, Z., Chen, B., Wang, J., Kim, J.: Decentralized energy management system for networked microgrids in grid-connected and islanded modes. IEEE Trans. Smart Grid **7**(2), 1097–1105 (2016). https://doi.org/10.1109/TSG.2015.2427371

20. Wang, Z., Chen, B., Wang, J., Kim, J., Begovic, M.M.: Robust optimization based optimal DG placement in microgrids. IEEE Trans. Smart Grid **5**(5), 2173–2182 (2014). https://doi.org/10.1109/TSG.2014.2321748
21. Yang, H., et al.: Operational planning of electric vehicles for balancing wind power and load fluctuations in a microgrid. IEEE Trans. Sustain. Energy **8**(2), 592–604 (2017). https://doi.org/10.1109/TSTE.2016.2613941
22. Zhang, H., Zhao, D., Gu, C., Li, F.: Bilevel economic operation of distribution networks with microgrid integration. J. Renew. Sustain. Energy **7**(2), 023120 (2015). https://doi.org/10.1063/1.4917556. https://doi.org/10.1063/1.4917556
23. Zhang, Z., Wang, J., Ding, T., Wang, X.: A two-layer model for microgrid real-time dispatch based on energy storage system charging/discharging hidden costs. IEEE Trans. Sustain. Energy **8**(1), 33–42 (2017). https://doi.org/10.1109/TSTE.2016.2577040
24. Zia, M.F., Elbouchikhi, E., Benbouzid, M.: Microgrids energy managementsystems: a critical review on methods, solutions, and prospects. Appl. Energy **222**, 1033–1055 (2018). https://doi.org/10.1016/j.apenergy.2018.04.103. http://www.sciencedirect.com/science/article/pii/S0306261918306676
25. Zou, H., Mao, S., Wang, Y., Zhang, F., Chen, X., Cheng, L.: A survey of energy management in interconnected multi-microgrids. IEEE Access **7**, 72158–72169 (2019). https://doi.org/10.1109/ACCESS.2019.2920008

Mining Network Security Holes Based on Data Flow Analysis in Smart Grid

Yang Li[1(✉)], Xiaohua Liu[2], Lixin Zhang[2], Wenbin Guo[2], and Qian Guo[3]

[1] State Grid Xinjiang Electric Power Research Institute, Xinjiang, China
455508995@qq.com
[2] State Grid Xinjiang Electric Power Co., Ltd., Xinjiang, China
{liuxiaohua,zhanglixin,guowenbin}@xj.sgcc.com.cn
[3] Global Energy Internet Research Institute Ltd., Nanjing, China
guoqian@geiri.sgcc.com.cn

Abstract. With the popularity of mobile terminals and the sharp increase in network data traffic, the problem of security loopholes has become increasingly prominent. The traditional vulnerability detection methods can no longer meet the demands for detection efficiency. In order to satisfy the high requirements on network security in the era of big data, the vulnerability mining technology is extremely urgent. This paper describes the current situation and introduces relevant security technology and algorithm in smart grid. The decision tree algorithm is selected as the basic algorithm of big data security technology. Through the test, the missing alarm rate and false alarm rate are simulated experimentally. We obtain the results of experiments by controlling variables, which proves that our algorithm can effectively detect IP scanning, Port scanning and other attacks.

Keywords: Big data · Data analysis · Vulnerability detection · Smart grid

1 Introduction

With the popularity of mobile terminals, the network data traffic has increased dramatically, information transmission rate is faster, and security vulnerabilities have become increasingly prominent. In order to satisfy the needs of network security in the era of big data and the requirements of in-depth mining of security vulnerabilities, it is necessary to design a system model combined with big data analysis in smart grid.

This article mainly describes vulnerability mining and detection technology, including three main points: common types of vulnerabilities, exploits and classification of exploits [1]. It also includes big data security analysis technologies. In addition, this paper also introduces the relevant algorithm in detail. During the use of the system, it is inevitable to encounter related attacks, and the security

Supported by State Grid Xinjiang Electric Power Co., Ltd.

D.-J. Deng et al. (Eds.): SGIoT 2019, LNICST 324, pp. 57–71, 2020.
https://doi.org/10.1007/978-3-030-49610-4_5

scanning is a method to simulate it. The security scanning is tested with the data set, and the system tested by this method has a certain defense performance, which has been able to preliminarily complete the relevant security work.

If the source code of the software can be known, we can use this method. By scanning the source code, we find the existence of security vulnerabilities, which can be targeted at the vulnerability of the source code modification. Source code scanning is a significant part of the programmer's job. However, a system code may be too large, manual operation may have considerable difficulty. The main contributions of this paper are listed as follows.

(1) We show the detailed description of the big data security analysis platform, as well as related algorithms, such as decision tree, and the relevant algorithm simulation test.
(2) We test the accuracy of the decision tree and a series of simulation of it.
(3) We present a bold conjecture of the future development of the related technologies mentioned in this paper and improvements to the subsequent related work of the algorithm are proposed.

The remainder of this paper is organized as follows. The Sect. 2 briefly introduces the related technologies involved in the main content of this paper. The Sect. 3 explains the relevant knowledge and algorithms of the big data security analysis platform. The Sect. 4 introduces the system model in detail. The Sect. 5 explains the design idea of the model. The Sect. 6 introduces the function of decision tree in mining security vulnerability based on data flow. The Sect. 7 analyzes the accuracy of the decision tree and carry out a series of simulation tests for it. The Sect. 8 concludes this work and make plans for the future.

2   Related Work

The process of exploiting vulnerability is to exploit the vulnerability in the computer system. Attackers use such vulnerabilities to achieve the desired purpose. The process and classification of vulnerability exploitation are described in detail.

In order to discover network vulnerabilities, attackers can use vulnerability information to obtain website user information and gain the entire website [2]. The basic process of exploitation is as follows: Scan the target site; Scan the target website with professional vulnerability detection software; Scan for known vulnerabilities [3].

The main detection content includes the system version type, relevant data services, and the system external port Settings. The obtained scan results are analyzed, which find the location of the vulnerability and its use.

Classification of common exploitation is shown as follows:

SQL Injection: A common approach is to inject SQL commands into the relevant pages. In this way, the original instruction can't be executed and the injected instruction can be run, thus entering into the vulnerability of the database, destroying the content of the database and the structure of the database [4].

XSS Cross-Site Scripting Attack: Similar to SQL injection. It is a method of injecting HTML. XSS can modify web pages and implant malicious scripts. The altered web page controls the browser with HTML statements when the user is using it [5]. The attacker can use the modified browser to steal the data stream related to the session, and through the data stream analysis, obtain the user's account password and change the appearance of the page.

Cross Site Request Forgery CSRF: The attacker interferes with the browser by forgery, so that the browser considers the intrusion site to be the previous authentication site, and the intrusion site obtains the corresponding operation authority. Authentication requests can only be made by the browser, but they may not be made by the user himself, and may be forged browser requests [6].

Click Hijacking: This is an attack method that uses the limitation of human senses to achieve the purpose. The main approach is to overlay the web page with an invisible HTML frame called an iframe. Since the iframe is not visible, the user mistakenly thinks it is a normal website for operation. In the operation process, the iframe will obtain the user's relevant account and password data through the operation of identifying the user [7].

Any File Upload Vulnerability: File upload vulnerability is mainly caused by the system is not strict screening. When uploading a file, the attributes of the file are not specified in the code [8]. An attacker can access any file on the web by changing its properties.

3 Preliminaries

In this section, we will present some preliminaries used in big data security analysis.

3.1 Big Data Security Analysis Technology

Big data analysis technology has gradually entered the field of security. We can use the big data analysis platform to collect data. In addition, we can use it for further analysis. By collecting and following up, we build a complete set of patterns [9]. This mode can effectively solve related security problems and maintain network security. Big data security analysis can also be combined with a variety of other technologies such as artificial intelligence [10].

In order to enable the platform to detect security issues more efficiently [11]. The shortcoming of the traditional detection method is solved and we need to continue to innovate better detection technology. We can adopt the related technology of artificial intelligence to improve such defects.

It is obviously to see from this diagram that the platform is an evolving hierarchy and the data flow is a gesture of directional movement. At the same time, it has feedback and adjustment in the platform. This also makes our platform more adaptable to some other scenarios, which means that the platform is more resistant and has a wider scope. In addition, big data security analysis platform needs to do some conditions to be able to be an excellent system [12]. First, you need a quick fix. Large data backlogs can cause serious network problems if they are not processed in a timely manner [13]. Then, accuracy is also important. If there are a lot of data errors, the security will not be guaranteed. At the same time, there will be problems in related data transmission and subsequent processing will be affected.

3.2   Application and Platform of Big Data Security

With the development of big data analysis technology, in the field of network security, big data analysis technology has been applied to a number of specific security work [14].

Application of big data analysis based on security log. The core idea of this application is the use of logs. Identify a potential common denominator through relevant statistical behavior [15]. According to the statistical results to find out the relevant safety rules, according to the rules to establish abnormal behavior model. Through the security model to apply to the actual, found the relevant holes, and can be improved model processing [16].

Advanced persistent threat attack is also known as Advanced Persistent Threat (APT) attack [17]. The APT attack has the characteristics of continuous attack and the main function is to steal the core data. It can bypass the detection of traditional protection methods and exist in the system for a long time. We can detect the data in the system through big data analysis technology, and obtain relevant abnormal data for analysis [18]. Through big data security analysis, threat perception can be improved and APT attacks can be detected and organized in a timely manner. Detection methods based on traditional feature analysis and insufficient to find new vulnerability attacks. So we need to use big data security analysis technology to protect the system. And through the intelligent system platform mining vulnerability use behavior. Currently, there are several commonly used security analysis algorithms in the field of big data security [19]:

(1) **Decision Tree Algorithm**. Decision tree algorithm is a method to approximate the value of discrete function. It is a typical classification method, the steps are divided into two steps. The first step is to generate a decision tree by processing sample data and induction algorithm based on corresponding rules. The second step is to classify and process the data by using the generated decision tree. The essence of it is to represent a series of rules for data processing in the form of binary tree. Data is traversed from the root node of the decision tree to the leaf node until it reaches the terminal, and classification is completed.

(2) **Naive Bayesian Model**. Naive bayesian model is a very accurate model in mathematics. However, the naive bayesian algorithm is simpler than the decision tree algorithm and the data integrity cannot be guaranteed. But naive bayesian model is more accurate in classification. Naive bayesian model is only suitable for small amount of data, and is inferior to decision tree model in large data analysis.

4   System Model

In this section, we will analyze system model for mining security holes in smart grid environment based on data flow analysis.

The vulnerability detection technology currently used in the society has great limitations in the era of big data explosion. Faced with massive data in the era of big data, we are bound to add network interface and network equipment to meet the detection requirements of massive data. This paper focuses on the above problems and proposes detection methods for big data security analysis [20]. And it mainly describes the construction of algorithm environment required by relevant experiments and the configuration of relevant parameters. The relevant steps of the experiment and parameters are introduced in detail, which is apparently to find that in the analysis of data flow, the original algorithm can achieve less false positives. It shows that the algorithm can satisfy a preliminary analysis function of data flow.

Big data analysis application based on data flow. We know that traffic is generated in network communication. Our application is built on the idea that behavior generates traffic. We set up a detection system for the nodes of the traffic flow in the network, through the analysis of the platform. Identify data streams that differ from normal traffic to complete the search for potential vulnerabilities. This model distinguish abnormal data and normal data, then carry out multidimensional analysis of abnormal data and establish relevant exception handling model to deal with the subsequent attack. This method can be used to exploit Web vulnerability, attack detection, scan attack and denial of service attack detection. Traffic analysis also allows for other aspects of the system, such as user behavior analysis. Figure 1 shows a system model for mining security holes in smart grid.

Big data analysis technology has gradually entered the field of security. We can use the big data analysis platform to collect data. In addition, we can use it for further analysis. By collecting and following up, we build a complete set of patterns. This mode can effectively solve the relevant security problems, so as to maintain network security. Big data security analysis can also be combined with a variety of other technologies such as artificial intelligence.

Current big data analysis methods are mainly based on distributed architecture to process massive data, and then match with the known database contents. After matching, detection, analysis and early warning of stored attacks in the database, the core of big data security analysis method based on self-updating threat intelligence database is to collect valuable intelligence to make up for the defects of traditional database.

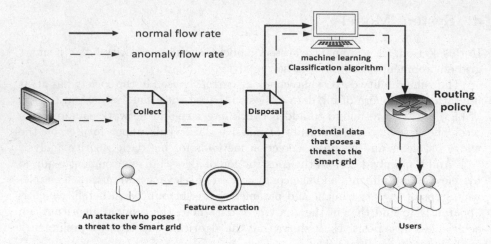

Fig. 1. A system model for mining security holes in smart grid.

5   System Design

The detection system is mainly composed of two parts: feature extraction and big data security analysis platform.

5.1   System Design Based on Big Data Detection

Feature Analysis: The main content of feature analysis is to analyze the related attributes of known data. After extraction, the attack behavior is classified from a series of factors such as traffic, behavior and attack mode. Feature extraction is the first step of data analysis [21]. Through feature analysis, we can more easily find the same rule of data flow. We use this common ground to further process the data. This process involves the screening of relevant redundant invalid data and classification of important data.

Big Data Security Analysis Platform: This module is the core module of big data security analysis [22]. It utilizes Spark-streaming platform and adopts decision tree classification. The algorithm analyzes the data obtained in one step, establishes the abnormal mechanism, and classifies the massive data. The classified data will distinguish between normal traffic and abnormal traffic, which will be assigned to different big data analysis modules for processing.

The big data security analysis platform is mainly divided into three levels: the collection layer is mainly responsible for sorting out the data in the network and extracting characteristic information, that is, useful information. Through the collection layer, the data to be processed by the big data platform is preliminarily reduced to facilitate the subsequent data processing. While the acquisition layer is working, we can do some preliminary processing on the data package. Based on the properties of the packet, the core data stream is saved and invalid data is discarded. After the data is preliminarily processed, the processed data is sent to the next layer for sorting. The main software of the finishing layer is distributed kafka system. The system receives the request from the upper level, organizes and stores the data stream, and waits for the data to make the next application call. In addition, the collation layer can also act as a buffer for the computing layer. The computing layer is mainly responsible for the calculation of mass data, and the classification algorithm is used here. This layer adopts Spark-streaming platform for streaming processing requirements. Decision tree algorithm is simple and easy to understand, which processes a large number of data, efficient and so on. By analyzing the potential security vulnerability of smart grid, we analyze and design the vulnerability mining model. Figure 2 shows the potential security threats in smart grid.

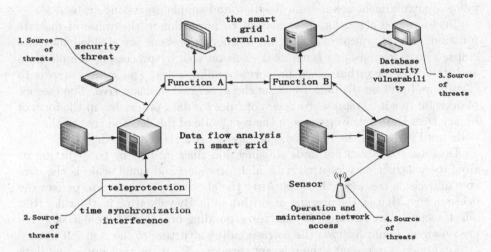

Fig. 2. Potential security threats in vulnerability mining design in smart grid.

5.2 Feature Extraction

Due to the massive data, we need to classify and process the big data first, so as to distinguish the normal traffic from the abnormal traffic. The steps for data classification generally have two parts. The first step is to classify data of known types according to relevant attributes and category relationships to obtain relevant data model. The data model is the feature model. The attributes used in the relevant classification are called eigenvalues. Second, after the establishment of the feature model, we can use the model to classify the new data and use the created vector model to classify and process data of unknown types. The accuracy of classification model is an embodiment of the accuracy of feature extraction. Common classification algorithms include decision tree classification and neural network classification [23].

6   Decision Tree Algorithm

Big data analysis technology has gradually entered the field of security. We can use the big data analysis platform to collect data. In addition, we can use it for further analysis. By collecting and following up, we build a complete set of patterns [24]. This mode can effectively solve the relevant security problems so as to maintain network security. Big data security analysis can also be combined with a variety of other technologies such as artificial intelligence. Decision tree algorithm is an important embodiment of big data security analysis and artificial intelligence [25]. In order to make the analysis more accurate, data analysis needs the support of multiple data. The required content is data traffic and relevant local log. For the obtained data, we can use Spark-streaming for processing. The calculations are then performed using Spark's own system. Flume used in the follow-up experiment is a data acquisition and simple processing system.

Decision tree algorithm is a method to approximate the value of discrete function. It is a typical classification method, the steps are divided into two steps. The first step is to generate a decision tree by processing sample data and induction algorithm based on corresponding rules. The second step is to classify and process the data by using the generated decision tree. The essence of decision tree is to represent a series of rules for data processing in the form of binary tree. Data is traversed from the root node of the decision tree to the leaf node until it reaches the terminal, and classification is completed.

Decision tree algorithm finds classification rules in data by constructing it. How to construct decision tree with high precision and small scale is the core step of decision tree algorithm [26]. After the above steps, we need to perfect the decision tree, that is, the pruning algorithm of it. By validating it, the rules that affect accuracy are removed, i.e. the corresponding branches of the decision tree are removed. Figure 3 shows the corresponding structure of the decision tree.

Leaf node N represents the relevant category. M_0 is the root node, and data processing starts from M_0 and $cond_{ij}$ is the relevant classification rule. In other words, we need to construct it with three conditions: data set, attribute set and attribute selection rule.

The construction of the decision tree is shown as follows:

Step 1: Construct a root node M. The classification or regression target of all nodes should be defined in the root node. The root node and the child node are opposite, that is, the child node is split from the root node according to a certain rule, and then the child node continues to split as a new root node until it cannot be split. The root node has no parent.

Step 2: If all the data in data set A have the same class index (denoted as class B), that is, all the sample data conform to rule B according to rule B. We'll just label M as B and return M.

Step 3: If all the data in data set A do not conform to the corresponding rules, that is, the class mark is different from all the class marks, then we mark M as the leaf node as the class mark with the most data, and A no longer performs classification calculation and returns M [27].

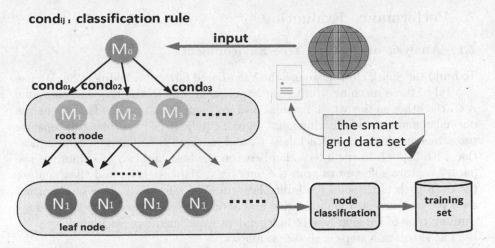

Fig. 3. Decision tree architecture applied to smart grid environment.

Step 4: The attribute selection algorithm is invoked to select the most accurate classification rule. Through this algorithm, the most accurate attributes of the classification are obtained, and subtrees of this category are required to belong to only one category as far as possible [28]. Entropy and index are commonly used to test the method of impurity. The test method of entropy is shown in formula:

$$Info(D) = -\sum_{i=1}^{n} p_i \log_2(p_i),\qquad(1)$$

where n represents the total number of class B, P_i represents the probability that the data in A belongs to B_i, and the value of i ranging from 1 to n indicates the number of classes of these discrete variables. P_i is the probability that any sample data is class B. And Info of D is what we call entropy. If we have a property called R, R has n equals k values. Then we can divide the samples in D into $n = k$, and the entropy value formula after classification is shown in formula:

$$Info_R(D) = -\sum_{j=1}^{k} \frac{|D_j|}{|D|} Info(D_j).\qquad(2)$$

This section mainly introduces the relevant big data security analysis platform program overview, including the big data security analysis platform related to some of the structure. At the same time this section chooses the decision tree algorithm to carry on the simulation experiment. The construction of decision tree is completed by simulation experiment, and the accuracy of the decision tree is also calculated. It also describes how to use entropy to calculate the accuracy of the relevant tree.

7 Performance Evaluation

7.1   Analysis of Decision Tree Environment

To build the Spark cluster, we use the Yarn-based farthest scheduler [29]. We use A total of three machines during the experiment, one as the host and we name it C, the other as the attack machine and we name it A, and the last one as the normal communication machine and we name it B. Brief experimental steps: we use attack machine A to attack host C, and machine B has normal communication with host C. In the interaction between the host and two machines, we use packet capture software to grab the interactive data packets, and then analyze the data packets through the built platform. The false alarm rate of abnormal data packets during communication and attack are calculated, and the average running time of three groups of independent experiments is calculated.

The simulation steps is shown as follows.

Step 1: Attack machine A and normal communication machine B access host C at the same time to ensure smooth communication.
Step 2: We use the packet capture software for packet capture.
Step 3: Data collation and start Kafka module.
Step 4: Import Kafka package into the program to be run and submit it to spark cluster for calculation in the form of spark-submit.

7.2   Simulation Results

We set the time window to 160 s and recorded the missing alarm rate of IP scanning, Port scanning and FIN scanning (Table 1).

Table 1. The set of parameter results.

Parameter	IP	Port	FIN
False Alarm Rate	0.5%	1.7%	1.7%
Missing Report Rate	0.7%	1.3%	2.4%

It is obviously to see from the above tables that the alarm rate and false alarm rate related to the decision tree algorithm are simulated by means of data simulation experiment. We get three sets of experimental results and find that the data obtained from the experiment showed that the alarm rate is about 1% and the false alarm rate is about 1.5%. This proves that our algorithm can be capable of big data security analysis of data screening.

7.3   Performance Analysis

We simulate the missing alarm rate and false alarm rate of decision tree algorithm. The grab results are shown in the Figs. 4, 5, and 6:

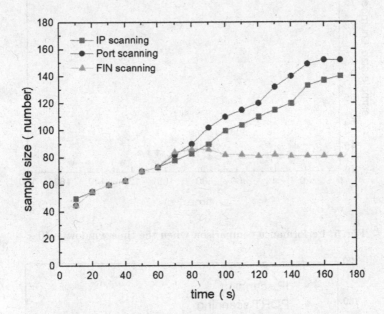

Fig. 4. Performance comparison when the time window is 20 s.

By means of data simulation experiment, this paper makes a simulation experiment on the missing alarm rate and false alarm rate of decision tree algorithm.

Through controlling variables, three groups of experimental results are obtained. The data obtained from the experiment shows that the alarm rate of IP scanning and Port scanning is about 1% and the false alarm rate is about 1.5%. We find that the missing alarm rate of the system is slightly higher than the false alarm rate, which is caused by the limitation of classification in the algorithm. Failure rate can be effectively reduced if the content of the original data set can be enlarged.

Through the integrated data of the three groups of tables, we can find that IP scanning attack has a better effect than other port attack and FIN scanning attack. The accuracy of Synchronize (SYN) attack and Domain Name System (DNS) attack needs to be improved. This proves that our algorithm can be capable of big data security analysis of data screening.

In conclusion, the experimental algorithm has a low false alarm rate, fast processing time and good performance against this kind of attack. Through this experiment, we find that big data has a high detection capability against several

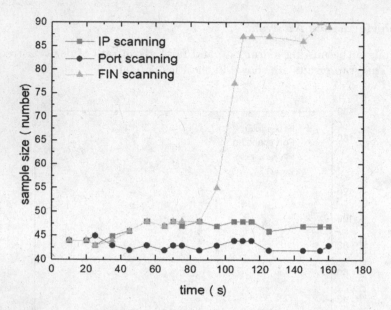

Fig. 5. Performance comparison when the time window is 40 s.

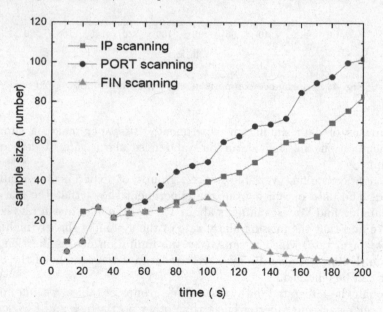

Fig. 6. Performance comparison when the time window is 120 s.

attack technologies in the above table. Compared with traditional vulnerability detection technology, big data security analysis technology has lower alarm rate and false alarm rate.

Through the experimental simulation, it is obviously to find that the original algorithm can achieve less false positives and less false positives. This shows that the algorithm can satisfy a preliminary analysis function of data flow.

This section conducts a simulation experiment on the missing alarm rate and false alarm rate related to decision tree algorithm by means of data simulation experiment. After controlling for variables, we got three sets of experimental results. We find that the data obtained from the experiment showed that the alarm rate was about 1% and the false alarm rate was about 1.5%. We are able to distinguish normal data and abnormal data accurately through the test of sample data.

8   Conclusion and Feature Work

In this paper, we propose an effective method of mining network security vulnerabilities based on data flow analysis technology. In order to improve the security of smart grid data transmission, we introduce the decision tree algorithm into the data transmission environment of smart grid and adopt more accurate vulnerability detection mechanism to ensure network security. In addition, we also demonstrate the characteristics of low alarm rate and false alarm rate by using decision tree algorithm for data flow analysis. This proves that our algorithm has the performance of big data security analysis. We also have some shortcomings which will be corrected in the future work. For example, if a user provides wrong information, they cannot be effectively found, so we need to design a scheme to distinguish them.

References

1. Hu, R.: Key technology for big visual data analysis in security space and its applications. In: 2016 International Conference on Advanced Cloud and Big Data (CBD), vol. 3, no. 4, p. 333 (2016)
2. Yu, J., Wang, K., Li, P., Xia, R., Guo, S., Guo, M.: Efficient trustworthiness management for malicious user detection in big data collection. In: IEEE Transactions on Big Data, October 2017
3. Albu, A.: From logical inference to decision trees in medical diagnosis. In: E-Health and Bioengineering Conference (EHB). Sinaia **2017**, 65–68 (2017)
4. Park, K.: On the effectiveness of route-based packet filtering for distributed DoS attack prevention in power-law internets. In: 2018 ACM SIGCOMM Computer Communication Review, December 2018
5. laski, J., Stanley, W.: Software verification and analysis. In: 2018 2nd IEEE Conference on Energy Internet and Energy System Integration (EI2), Springer, London (2018) https://doi.org/10.1007/978-1-84882-240-5
6. Wang, K., et al.: Wireless big data computing in smart grid. IEEE Wireless Communi. **24**(2), 58–64 (2017)
7. Wang, K., Du, M., Maharjan, S., Sun, Y.: Strategic honeypot game model for distributed denial of service attacks in the smart grid. IEEE Trans. Smart Grid **8**(5), 2474–2482 (2017)

8. Xu, C., Wang, K., Li, P., Xia, R., Guo, S., Guo, M.: Renewable energy-aware big data analytics in geo-distributed data centers with reinforcement learning. IEEE Tran. Network Sci. Eng. **7**, 205–215 (2018)
9. Amir, M.A.U.: Optimal specification of wave flume in confined space. In: 2016 International Conference on Information and Communication Technology (ICICTM), Kuala Lumpur, pp. 136–140 (2016)
10. Du, M., Wang, K., Xia, Z., Zhang, Y.: Differential privacy preserving of training model in wireless big data with edge computing. In: IEEE Transactions on Big Data, May 2018
11. Al-Shomrani, A., Yang, Y.M., Wang, X.: Quickest detection of false data injection attack in wide-area smart grids. IEEE Trans. Smart Grid **6**(6), 2725–2735 (2017)
12. Wang, K., Fathy, F., Jambi, K.: Policy enforcement for big data security. In: 2017 2nd International Conference on Anti-Cyber Crimes (ICACC), pp. 70–74. Abha (2017)
13. Burguera, I., Zurutuza, U.: Behavior-based Malware detection system for Android. In: Proceedings of the 1st ACM Workshop on Security and Privacy in Smartphones and Mobile Devices, pp. 15–26. ACM, Chicago (2011)
14. Xie, L., Zhang, X., Seifert, J.: A behavior-based malware detection system for cell-phone devices. In: Proceedings of the Third ACM Conference on Wireless Network Security, pp. 37–48. New Jersey, ACM (2010)
15. Gavankar, S.S., Sawarkar, S.D.: Eager decision tree. In: 2nd International Conference for Convergence in Technology (I2CT). Mumbai **2017**, 837–840 (2017)
16. Wang, K., Ouyang, Z., Krishnan, R., Shu, L., He, L.: A game theory based energy management system using price elasticity for smart grids. IEEE Trans. Ind. Inform. **11**(6), 1607–1616 (2015)
17. Al-Hoqani, W.M., Giampapa, J.A.: Difficulties of marking decision tree diagrams. Computing Conference. London **2017**, 1190–1194 (2017)
18. Wang, Y., Wang, K., Huang, H., Miyazaki, T., Guo, S.: Traffic and computation co-offloading with reinforcement learning in fog computing for industrial applications. IEEE Trans. Ind. Inform. **15**(2), 976–986 (2019)
19. Ignatov, D., Ignatov, A.: Decision stream: cultivating deep decision trees. In: 2017 IEEE 29th International Conference on Tools with Artificial Intelligence (ICTAI), Boston, MA, pp. 905–912 (2017)
20. Gao, M., Wang, K., He, L.: Probabilistic model checking and scheduling implementation of energy router system in energy internet for green cities. IEEE Trans. Ind. Inform. **14**(4), 1501–1510 (2018)
21. Kumar, R.: Development of synchronization system of two spark gaps. In: 2012 IEEE 5th India International Conference on Power Electronics (IICPE), Delhi, pp. 1–3 (2012)
22. Revathy, P., Mukesh, R.: Analysis of big data security practices. In: 2017 3rd International Conference on Applied and Theoretical Computing and Communication Technology (iCATccT), Tumkur, pp. 264–267 (2017)
23. Wang, K., Shao, Y., Xie, L., Wu, J., Guo, S.: Adaptive and fault-tolerant data processing in healthcare IoT based on fog computing. IEEE Transactions on Network Science and Engineering, July 2018
24. Lighari, S.N., Hussain, D.M.A.: Hybrid model of rule based and clustering analysis for big data security. In: 2017 First International Conference on Latest trends in Electrical Engineering and Computing Technologies (INTELLECT), Karachi, pp. 1–5 (2017)

25. Aljuhani, A., Alharbi, T.: Virtualized network functions security attacks and vulnerabilities. In: IEEE 7th Annual Computing and Communication Workshop and Conference (CCWC). Las Vegas, NV **2017**, 1–4 (2017)

26. Wang, K., Yu, J., Liu, X., Guo, S.: A pre-authentication approach to proxy reencryption in big data context. In: IEEE Transactions on Big Data, May 2017

27. Li, P., Min, X.: Accurate marking method of network attacking information based on big data analysis. In: 2019 International Conference on Intelligent Transportation, Big Data Smart City (ICITBS), Changsha, China, pp. 228–231 (2019)

28. Wang, K., Li, H., Maharjan, S., Zhang, Y., Guo, S.: Green energy scheduling for demand side management in the smart grid. IEEE Trans. Green Commun. Network. **2**(2), 596–611 (2018)

29. Nethercote, N., Seward, J.: A Framework for Heavyweight Dynamic Binary Instrumentation (2017)

Architecture and Network Design for Industrial Internet of Things

Manan Bawa, Dagmar Caganova[(✉)], and Natalia Hornakova

Faculty of Materials Science and Technology in Trnava Institute of Industrial Engineering and Management, Slovak University of Technology in Bratislava, Bottova 25, 917 01 Trnava, Slovakia

{manan.bawa,dagmar.caganova,natalia.hornakova}@stuba.sk

Abstract. The aim of the paper is to provide the best architecture and the most suitable network design for companies that are working in the space of Industrial Internet of Things. The architecture of internet hourglass model and method for selecting the Industrial Internet of Things network protocol is proposed and tested in this paper. The network design model is called as three-dimensional network design space which includes battery life, device data rate, and device to gateway range. Different industry accepted and globally available wireless network protocols are tested to define the best network protocol for Industrial Internet of Things. The hypothesis experiment and research results for the architecture model are directly implied to the practical benefits for industrial companies.

Keywords: Network design · Architecture · Industrial Internet of Things · Industrial management · Innovation

1 Introduction

Industrial Internet of Things (IIoT) is a network of connected devices like sensors, machines, smart devices, and other physical objects which tie to central cloud-based network servers. The network has the competence to monitor and control the functionality of the machines [1, 2]. The architecture and the framework for IIoT become a presidential requirement which defines the backbone for the IIoT system for all industrial enterprises.

IIoT based solutions has specific requirements for network communication like range, power consumption, etc. There are many network protocols which are available in the market for industrial applications depending upon the different network coverage area, are shown in the Fig. 1 [2].

This paper concentrates on the network connectivity and architecture for IIoT deve-lopment. Furthermore, the paper proposes the three-dimensional network design model to find the best network protocol and provide hypothesis results for selecting the ideal architecture model that will work for different IIoT applications across different industrial companies.

D.-J. Deng et al. (Eds.): SGIoT 2019, LNICST 324, pp. 72–81, 2020.
https://doi.org/10.1007/978-3-030-49610-4_6

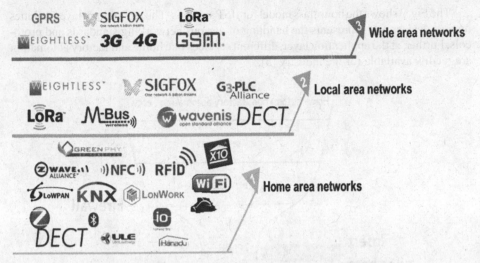

Fig. 1. IIoT wireless protocols [3, 13]

2 Architecture Model for Industrial Internet of Things

The architecture model for the IIoT can be based upon the hourglass model of the internet as it fulfils stringent IIoT requirements. The Fig. 2 shows the three key aspects for selecting an architectural model [4]:

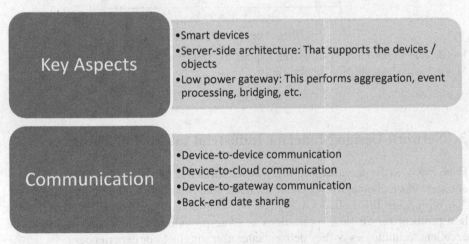

Fig. 2. Key aspects to consider while selecting IIoT architecture

IIoT is a complex system as it involves a lot of smarter, smaller sized, and hetero-geneous devices which interconnect between the technology and the application layer. Furthermore, the complexity quotient is increased because of networking technology like wireless, LAN, RFID or LTE as they operate and function at different ranges [5].

The Fig. 3 shows the hourglass model for IIoT systems. The technology layer includes diverse devices and represents the handling of various networking standards and protocols. Further, at the application layer, different services like home and factory automation are readily available for the industry [5].

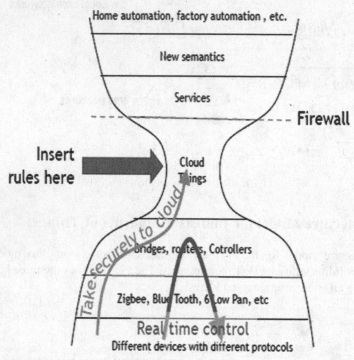

Fig. 3. IIoT architecture. Source: The Internet of Things: Roadmap to a Connected World, Massachusetts Institute of Technology 2016

3   Network Design Model for Industrial Internet of Things

From Fig. 1, in the previous section it was determined that there are wide range of different networks technologies which are available like Bluetooth Low Energy, 6LoWPAN, 3G, WiFi, LTE, IEEE 802.15.4, ZigBee, etc. Therefore, it becomes difficult to find the best protocol for all IIoT applications as some provide high performance, others are excellent technologies or they deliver better user interfaces or experiences.

The proposed network design model for the IIoT applications is referred as the three-dimensional network design model. This model will help the industrial enterprises to easily choose the network protocol for their Industrial IoT development. The model is divided into three axes as shown in the Fig. 4. The first dimension on the x-axis is the battery life, the second dimension on the y-axis is the device data rate or the duty cycle, and the third dimension on the z-axis is the device to gateway range [6].

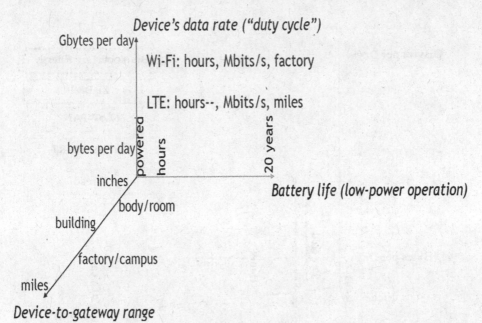

Fig. 4. Three-dimensional network design model. Source: The Internet of Things: Roadmap to a Connected World, Massachusetts Institute of Technology 2016

3.1 Comparison of Wireless Network Protocols

The selected protocols for the comparison were based upon their popularity in the industrial environment and their wide range for fulfilling the requirements for IIoT applications. Further, these protocols were placed against the three-dimensional network design model and compared. The comparison results are shown in the Fig. 5:

- **Thread:** The advantage is that it is low-power and low-cost over other protocols. Application includes mobile, device to device communication and smart home [7].
- **ZigBee:** Based on the IEEE 802.15.4 link layer and operates in 2.4 GHz ISM bank. The network layer is based upon mesh topology [8]. The applications include smart homes, smart building and home automation.
- **Wireless HART:** It is based on IEEE 802.15.4, designed for industrial applications processes – providing access to diagnostics, configuration and process data [8].
- **Bluetooth Low Energy (BLE):** It is very popular in diverse applications ranging from automobiles, fitness, audio, video, heart rate monitor, etc.
- **6LoWPAN:** Acronym for IPv6 over Low Power Wireless Personal Area Networks. A mesh network topology, large area network, reliable communication and low power consumption [7].

The comparison results are in many magnitudes of ranges that fits different technologies. Each technology has their own benefit, as some protocols have higher battery life; others have better device to gateway range, or device duty cycle. One of the best practices

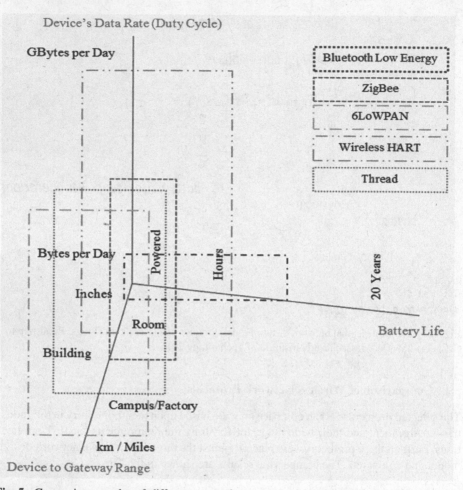

Fig. 5. Comparison results of different network protocol against the three-dimensional IIoT network design model

is to place the specific IIoT requirements against the three dimensional graph and find out the best protocol technology which met all the IIoT applications requirements [6]. Another best practice is to select any given technology or protocol and place it against the three dimension model to identify if the IIoT application requirements are satisfied.

4 Results for Industrial Internet of Things Architecture Model

To evaluate the best architecture model for the IIoT systems, the previous and current architecture models were studied and tested under different testing parameters. Furthermore, a survey was conducted across a multinational IIoT based company which specializes in industrial space including energy sector, heavy machinery, and oil and gas industry. 117 employees from 20 countries participated in the survey to discuss if internet hourglass model is the best architecture model for IIoT. The Figs. 6 and 7, provides the survey results.

How many IoT application do you work on within one month?
117 responses

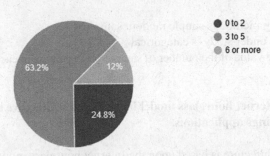

Fig. 6. How many IoT applications do the participants work in one month

The survey results showed that about 63% employees said they work with 3 to 5 application in one month. About 25% replied they work with 0 to 2 IIoT applications and whereas only 12% said they use or develop 6 or more IIoT application in each month.

Which network protocol you use for these applications
117 responses

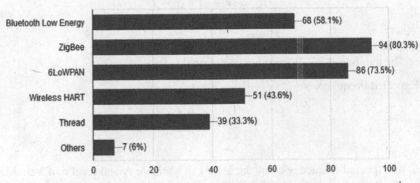

Fig. 7. Network protocol used by the company

The choices provided of all the protocols referenced in this paper were based upon the popularity of the network protocols in IIoT environment and in industrial companies. The option "others" were added if the employees do not use the above mentioned protocols in their organizations. The popular choice included all the protocols which were recommend in this paper, in decreasing order – ZigBee (80%), 6LoWPAN (74%), Bluetooth Low Energy (58%), Wireless HART (44%) and Thread (33%). Only 6% belonged to the others option. All these protocols are architecturally derived from the hourglass model and it holds true to evaluate that the internet hourglass model is the best architectural model for IIoT.

4.1 Testing

The "Chi-Square Goodness of Fit Test" method was used to prove the test, since the sample fulfilled the following basic requirements [9]:

- The sampling method is simple random sampling
- The variable under study is categorical
- The expected value of the number of sample observations in each level of the variable is at least 5.

Hypothesis: **Internet hourglass model is the best architecture model for Industrial Internet of Things applications.**

- H0: IIoT architecture is based upon the Internet hourglass model

To evaluate this hypothesis:

- Q1: How many IoT applications do you work on within one month?
- Q2: Which network protocol you use for these applications

Parameters used:
Degrees of Freedom (DF):

$$DF = (r - 1) * (c - 1) \tag{1}$$

Where:
r: Number of levels for one categorical variable
c: The number of levels for other categorical variable

Expected Frequencies:

$$E_{r,c} = \frac{(n_r * n_c)}{n} \tag{2}$$

Where:
$E_{r,c}$: Expected frequency count for lever r of Variable A and level c of Variable B
n_r: Total number of sample observations at lever r of Variable A
n_c: Total number of sample observations at lever c of Variable B in the total sample.

Test statistic:

$$x^2 = \sum \frac{(O_{r,c} - E_{r,c})^2}{E_{r,c}} \tag{3}$$

Where:
$O_{r,c}$: Observed frequency count at lever r of Variable A and level c of Variable B
$E_{r,c}$: Expected frequency count at level r of Variable A and level c of Variable B

Table 1. Observed values for Q1 and Q2

Q2: How many IoT applications do you work on wihthin one month?	Q5: Which network protocol you use for these applications						
Q2 and Q5	Bluetooth low energy	ZigBee	6LoWPAN	Wireless HART	Thread	Others	SUM
0 to 2	5	7	7	4	3	4	29
3 to 5	14	19	18	10	8	6	74
6 or More	2	3	3	2	1	1	14
Total	21	29	28	16	12	11	117

P-value:

The P-value is the probability of observing a sample statistic as extreme as the test statistic. Since the test statistic is a Chi-square, we need to assess the probability associated with the test statistics. This is done using the degrees of freedom [10, 11] (Table 1). Degree of Freedom from Eq. (1):

$$DF = (3 - 1) * (6 - 1) = 10$$

Expected frequencies from Eq. (2) (Table 2):
Test statistics x^2 from Eq. (3) (Table 3):

Table 2. Expected values for Q1 and Q2

Q2: How many IoT applications do you work on within one month?	Q5: Which network protocol you use for these applications						
Q2 and Q5	Bluetooth low energy	ZigBee	6LoWPAN	Wireless HART	Thread	Others	SUM
0 to 2	5.21	7.19	6.94	3.97	2.97	2.73	29
3 to 5	13.28	18.34	17.21	10.12	7.59	6.96	74
6 to More	2.51	3.47	3.35	1.91	1.44	1.32	14
Total	21	29	28	16	12	11	117

Table 3. Test values for Q1 and Q2

Q2: How many IoT applications do you work on within one month?	Q5: Which network protocol you use for these applications						
Q2 and Q5	Bluetooth low energy	ZigBee	6LoWPAN	Wireless HART	Thread	Others	SUM
0 to 2	0.0081	0.0049	0.0005	0.0003	0.0002	0.5948	0.6089
3 to 5	0.0388	0.0236	0.0048	0.0014	0.0222	0.1317	0.2225
6 to More	0.1047	0.0637	0.0367	0.0038	0.1323	0.0760	0.4171
Total	0.1515	0.0922	0.0419	0.0055	0.1547	0.8025	1.2485

The calculated degree of freedom is 10. The calculated testing criteria or the Chi-Square value is 1.2485 and p is 0.9995 [11, 12]. Comparing the calculated testing values against the critical value, it is observed that the calculated testing value is less (1.2485 < 18.307). The used level of significance was 0.05.

Therefore, it is concluded that H0 is accepted; hence proving the internet hourglass model is the best architecture model for Industrial Internet of Things.

5   Conclusion

The proposed three-dimensional network design model for Industrial Internet of Things was studied and successfully placed against the popular industrial network protocols like Bluetooth Low Energy, ZigBee, Wireless HART, 6LowPAN, Thread, etc. The three-dimensional model consists of duty cycle, battery life, and device and gateway range. The best practices for using the network design for IIoT systems are:

- The network design for IIoT application is based on the terms of which technology or combinations of technology are the best suited for that particular IIoT application by placing the requirements.
- Take the three-dimensional models and place the preferred technology and see if it fits the requirements of the intended IIoT application.

Furthermore, the research objective of the paper was also to prove that the internet hourglass model is the best architectural model for the IIoT applications or systems, which was proved by conducting the survey and testing the hypothesis using the Chi-Square Goodness of Fit Test criteria.

Acknowledgements. This research was supported and funded by 030STU-4/2018 KEGA project titled "E-platform as basis for improving collaboration among universities and industrial enterprises in the area of education", with support of 2/0077/19 VEGA project titled "Work competencies in the context of Industry 4.0" and H2020 Nr. 873134 "Linking Research and Innovation for Gender Equality".

References

1. Shelby, Z., Bormannc, C.: 6LoWPAN: the Wireless Embedded Internet. Wiley, West Sussex (2009)
2. Bawa, M., Caganova, D., Szilva, I., Spirkova D.: Importance of internet of things and big data in building smart city and what would be its challenges. In: EAI International Conference on Mobility Opportunities in Danube Region, Bratislava, Slovakia (2015)
3. Caganova, D., Bawa, M., Sobrino, D.R.D., Saniuk, A.: Internet of Things and smart city, University of Zielona Góra, Poland (2017). ISBN 978-83-65200-07-5
4. Fremantle, P.: A Reference Architecture for the Internet of Things, White paper published in WSO2, Version 0.9.0 (2015)
5. Walewski, J. W., et al.: Internet-of-Things Architecture, Report on Project Deliverable D1.2 – Initial Architectural Reference Model for IoT. Project co-funded by the European Commission within the Seventh Framework Programme. Grant agreement number – 257521 (2011)
6. Balakrishnan, H.: The Internet of Things: Roadmap to a connected world, MIT Professional Education, Digital Programs, Massachusetts Institute of Technology, Cambridge, USA (2016)
7. Lethaby, N.: Wireless connectivity for the Internet of Things: One size does not fit all, paper published by Texas Instruments, SWRY010A, Texas, USA (2017)
8. Gerber, A.: Connecting all the things in the Internet of Things, paper published in the Developer Works magazine, issued by IBM, Article (2018). https://developer.ibm.com/articles/iot-lp101-connectivity-network-protocols/
9. Cagáňová, D., Szilva, I., Proposal of a Knowledge Management Tool for Tacit and Explicit Knowledge Capture within the Assembly Process. 1. vyd. Ostrava Amos, 118 s (2018). ISBN 978-80-906362-3-1
10. Columbia University, ccnmtl.columbia.edu (2016), Article http://ccnmtl.columbia.edu/projects/qmss/the_chisquare_test/about_the_chisquare_test.html
11. Szilva, I.: Increasing Efficiency of Assembly Process through Innovative KM Tool, Dissertation Thesis, Trnava, Slovak Technical University in Bratislava, MTF, Slovakia (2017)
12. Stanford, web.stanford.edu (2016). Article http://web.stanford.edu/class/psych252/cheatsheets/chisquare.html
13. Macaigne, G.: Sim-less Networks, The New Eldorado of M2M and Internet of Things, published in Invo360 (2014). https://www.inov360.com/en/sim-less-networks-the-new-eldorado-of-m2m-and-internet-of-things/

Applications and Technologies

Power Prediction via Module Temperature for Solar Modules Under Soiling Conditions

Salsabeel Shapsough(✉) , Rached Dhaouadi , Imran Zualkernan ,
and Mohannad Takrouri

American University of Sharjah, Sharjah, UAE
sshapsough@aus.edu

Abstract. The ability to predict the output power of remote solar modules is key to successful wide-scale adoption of solar power. However, solar power is a direct product of its environment and can vary vastly from one location to another. Predicting generated power for a specific facility requires monitoring the output of the solar modules in the context of ambient variables such as temperature, humidity, solar irradiance, air dust, and wind. This is especially challenging in areas where soiling is a significant environmental variable. Soiling particles such as sand and dust can shade segments of the solar module, thus effectively reducing the amount of solar irradiance absorbed and, consequently, the power produced. Measuring soiling particles requires expensive equipment that can increase the cost of running the facility and therefore lower the total output. However, dust can also serve as a cooling layer that can reduce the temperature of the solar module and to a certain extent, reduce overheating. This observation can be used to correlate the amount of dust accumulated on the surface of the panel with its temperature. In this work, the module temperature and power output of a clean module and a dusty module are observed using an Internet of Things monitoring system. The data is used to train various machine learning and deep learning algorithms to eventually predict the output of a soiled module over time using only its temperature and a reference clean module.

Keywords: Photovoltaic · Module temperature · Prediction · Machine learning

1 Introduction

Wide-scale deployment of solar power faces significant challenges due to the source's dependence on its environment. Environmental elements such as temperature, shading, wind, and soiling can cause the power yield to deviate significantly from expected values [1]; thus, making it more challenging to adopt the solar power as a reliable energy source. Artificial intelligence is key to overcoming such obstacles by providing tools to build models that make it possible to understand the behavior of solar modules out in the field, as well as generate short-term and long-term predictions to efficiently plan production by matching load to demand [2]. The first step to modeling solar power is understanding factors that have the most influence on modules in a given setting. As the significance of

D.-J. Deng et al. (Eds.): SGIoT 2019, LNICST 324, pp. 85–95, 2020.
https://doi.org/10.1007/978-3-030-49610-4_7

different elements may vary from one location to another, it is critical when modeling a solar facility to take into account its operating conditions as accurately as possible. This is where remote an in-situ monitoring comes in [3]. Building accurate models requires collection of a solar facility's output as well as context over a long period of time. However, since the cost of monitoring instrumentation can increase the cost of large-scale facilities and reduce the overall efficiency of production, the type of data collected should be considered carefully. Monitoring should focus on observing elements that have the most significant impact in that specific setting.

In desert areas, soiling represents the biggest obstacle to solar energy [4]. The presence of soil particles on the surface of the panel can influence its behavior. It is well-known that the accumulation of sand and dust particles on the surface of the panel can reduce the amount of solar irradiance absorbed by the panel, effectively reducing the output power [5]. One way to quantify the level of soil on the surface of a panel is by simulating panels through a glass plate and measuring the optical losses due to the dust accumulated on the plate [6, 7]. However, such studies become less feasible as the facility in question increases in scale as the distribution of the aerosol index (AI) varies spatially and temporally. Alternatively, several studies investigated the approximation of the soiling index using output power relative to meteorological conditions such as aerosol particle size [8], mechanics [9], and composition [10, 11]. While accuracy is relatively high in such works, the cost of the instrumentation required to perform such studies may exceed the benefit.

Most recent and existing work focuses instead on measuring the influence of soil particles. Commonly, the performance of a clean panel with a soiled one and use the loss percentage to calculate a "soiling index" [12] that is indicative of the soil accumulation on a soiled module's surface. The soiling index is then used to predict the power output of soiled modules given the module's temporal and environmental context. While soil's influence as a shading agent has been studied in numerous works, it has not yet been characterized as the complex phenomenon it is. For one, module's surface temperature is a function of solar irradiance absorbed by the module as well as ambient temperature [13]. By shading the module and reducing the amount of solar irradiance absorbed, the accumulation of soil on the surface of a module can interfere with heat transfer between the module and its environment and have a cooling effect [14]. The output of a solar module depends on the temperature of its cells as much as it depends on solar irradiance incidence. Standard Test Conditions (STC) denote temperature and irradiance values at which a module outputs maximum power. In desert areas, module overheating can significantly reduce the output of the module. Cooling due to soil accumulation, however, may have an opposite effect. It is therefore beneficial to investigate the correlation between soil's influence on module temperature and output power.

This work aims to investigate the relationship between soiling and module temperature, and their consequent influence on output power. First, a low-cost monitoring system using Internet of Thing technologies to remotely monitor the performance and context of solar module. The data collected over the period of ten weeks is then used to build various machine learning models to predict the output of a soiled module using only its temperature and a reference clean module.

2 Hardware Setup

The test setup consisted of two identical 100 W monocrystalline solar panels, shown in Fig. 1 (a). One was cleaned every week, while the other was left to gather dust and other soiling elements for ten weeks. The panels' performance and context were measured using an IoT-based monitoring system discussed in [15]. Performance was measured by performing IV tracing once every hour to extract the maximum power point, short circuit current, and open circuit voltage of each panel. The context, on the other hand, included the ambient temperature and solar irradiance. The module temperature was measured using twenty low-cost one-wire temperature sensors distributed across each module. While the sensors do not measure every single cell temperature, the twenty cells that were measure were selected as to cover each region of the module. The layout of the temperature sensors on the back of each panel is shown in Fig. 1 (b).

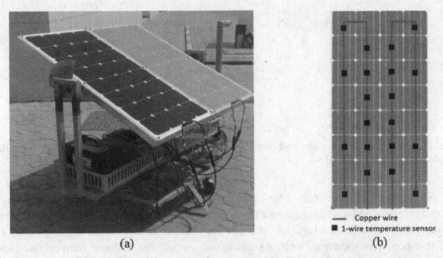

(a)   (b)

Fig. 1. (a) Test setup (b) one-wire temperature sensors layout

3 Data Analysis

At the end of the testing period, the dataset consisted of over 800 entries denoting the cell temperatures and power output of each panel, solar irradiance and ambient temperature readings, timestamp, and number of days since the beginning of the experiment. In the first phase of analysis, the average module temperature was calculated by averaging the individual cell temperatures. The behavior of individual cell temperatures will be explored in future works.

3.1 Soiling and Module Cooling

First, Fig. 2 shows the general trend in ambient temperature as well as the two modules' temperatures using all the readings observed during the test period, as well as with filtering out solar noon values. Solar noon refers to the time of the day where irradiance is at its highest value. It usually occurs between 12:00 pm and 01:00 pm and is a common method of studying module performance at maximum possible yield. Both figures show a general rise in temperatures as time goes by and the season progresses more towards summer (July). As the dusty panel was not clean at the beginning of the testing period, the temperature difference between the two panels appears early on as the dusty panel starts off with a slightly lower temperature.

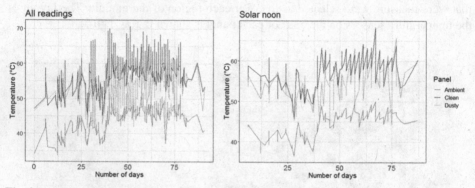

Fig. 2. Ambient, clean module, and dusty module temperatures vs. number of days since the beginning of the test period

Next, a heatmap was created for each panel which shows the distribution of average module reading and maximum power throughout the test period (Fig. 3). Given the level of dust accumulation is a function of time, the number of days since the beginning of the test period is shown as well. As discussed earlier, the ambient temperature, and consequently the modules' temperatures, increased with time. This is observable as most of the reading at the beginning are clustered around the 50 °C point but begin to shift towards 60 and 70 °C. Consequently, as the module overheats it also experiences a decrease in output power. While the shift is clear in the clean panel readings, the dusty panel exhibits a different trend. The maximum power decreases with time, while increase in temperature is generally less noticeable. While the decrease of power can be attributed to the accumulation of dusty which effectively lowers the amount of solar irradiance absorbed by the panel, it is likely that the dust also serves as a cooling mechanism which prevents the module overheat exhibited by the clean panel.

The relationship between ambient and each module's temperature can be furthered explored by running a correlation analysis. The dataset was first divided based on time of the day in order to eliminate time as a variable. As shown in Fig. 4, there is a strong correlation between ambient temperature and the clean module's temperature throughout the day.

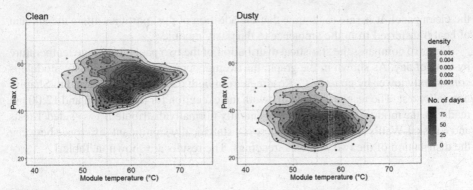

Fig. 3. Statistical distribution of average module temperature and maximum power for the clean and dusty panels

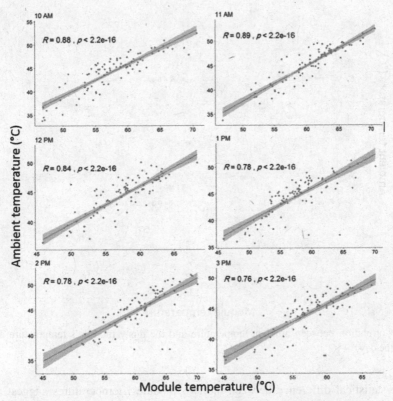

Fig. 4. Correlation between ambient temperature and the clean module's temperature at each hour of the day

Looking at the dusty panel readings in Fig. 5, however, shows that the correlation between the ambient temperature and the dusty module's temperature is not as strong as the clean panel. It is safe to assume that the addition of dust particles alters the amount of heat transferred from the ambience to the dusty module.

Figure 6 compares the statistical distribution of the two panels' average temperature by time of day. As shown in the graph, the average temperature of the dusty module is consistently lower by up to 6 °C. Readings from both panels were subjected to Shapiro normality test. The results showed that with the exception for the 3:00 pm and 12:00 pm readings, the module temperature was generally normally distributed. Two-sided T-tests and Kruskal-Wallis test showed that there is a statistically significant difference between the distribution of the two modules' readings. The results are shown in Table 1.

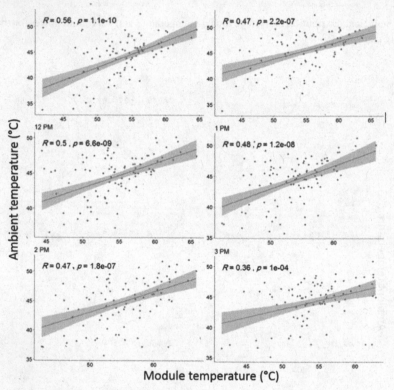

Fig. 5. Correlation between ambient temperature and the dusty module's temperature at each hour of the day

The statistical difference between the two modules' temperatures suggest that it might be possible to use the module temperature as an indication of dust levels. If true, it could be possible to use the difference in temperature between a dusty module and a clean one to predict the dusty module's output, if the clean module's temperature is known. Clean PV modules exhibit a fairly linear dependence on solar irradiance. This was confirmed in [16], where a linear regression model was used to predict the output of

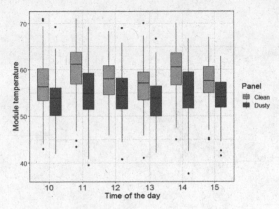

Fig. 6. Comparing statistical distribution of the two modules' temperatures by time of day

a clean module using only solar irradiance. Given a reference clean panel whose output and temperature are known, the goal is to approximate the output of a dusty module out in the field with low cost hardware and little and no interference with the dusty module's circuitry.

Table 1. Results of statistical analysis of the module temperature distributions

			10 am	11 am	12 pm	1 pm	2 pm	3 pm
Shapiro	Clean	W	0.982	0.980	0.977	0.992	0.988	0.979
		P_value	0.134	0.108	0.037	0.670	0.428	0.078
	Dusty	W	0.989	0.984	0.989	0.988	0.984	0.974
		P_value	0.472	0.225	0.461	0.325	0.196	0.029
T-test	Module temperature	T-value	5.143	8.636	NA	6.238	7.121	NA
		Df	220.03	211.1	NA	255.6	22.59	NA
		p-value	$6.0e - 7$	$1.4e - 15$	NA	$1.8e - 9$	$1.5e - 11$	NA
Kruskal-Wallis	Module temperature	Chi-squared	227	215	239	257	227	221
		df	171	165	183	191	173	169
		P_value	0.0027	0.0054	0.0034	0.0010	0.0037	0.0044

3.2 Power Prediction via Module Temperature

Several models were built in an attempt to predict the output of a dusty panel using a reference clean module and low-cost hardware at the dusty module's site. The input variables considered were the maximum power of a reference clean panel, the difference in temperature between the dusty and clean panels, the number of days, and time of the day. The structure of the neural network is shown in Fig. 7.

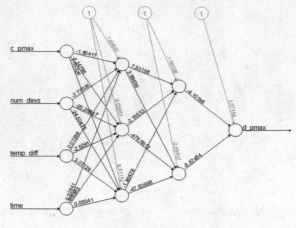

Error: 1.785687 Steps: 8020

Fig. 7. Neural network used to predict the output of a dusty panel

The training and testing were done via 10-fold cross validation. the dataset was divided into 10 random subsets, and each subset was used once to test while rest of the dataset was used to train for a total of 10 full training and testing runs. The process was also repeated 10 times to decrease bias. The average Root Mean Square Error (RMSE) and correlation coefficient (R) were calculated by averaging the statistics of all runs. Table 2 shows an evaluation of the models built to predict the maximum power of a dusty module using only its average temperature and information about a reference clean module.

Table 2. Results of running various machine learning algorithms to predict the maximum power point of a dusty module

	Back propagation neural network	Random forest	Random tree	Linear regression	Lazy IBK	Regression by discretization	Multilayer perceptron
R	0.8684	0.9846	0.9846	0.8407	0.9089	0.9461	0.8622
MAE	0.0572	0.0230	0.0125	0.0913	0.0477	0.0462	0.0837
RMSE	0.0735	0.0359	0.0355	0.1095	0.0859	0.0657	0.1039

As the table shows, the algorithms with the lowest root mean square error are the random trees and random forest, with an RMSE of 0.036 and 0.035, respectively. To compare with existing literature on power prediction, Table 3 presents a comparison of various models presented in literature. In addition to varying algorithms, a different assortment of context variable was used in each work. As shown in the table, the results achieved by the proposed model are comparable with other proposed models that utilize more elaborate context variables.

Table 3. Performance comparison of example models in literature for power prediction

Source	Inputs	Context	Algorithm	RMSE	MAE	R
[17]	Cumulative dust, temperature, humidity, module temperature, irradiance, dust, wind speed	N/S	Linear regression	0.074	0.050	0.926
	Temperature, module temperature, irradiance, dust	N/S	Linear regression	0.095	0.070	0.877
	Irradiance, wind speed, module temperature, temperature	N/S	Linear regression	0.094	0.069	0.878
	Cumulative dust, temperature, humidity, module temperature, irradiance, dust, wind speed	N/S	M5P tree	0.070	0.048	0.934
	Temperature, module temperature, irradiance, dust	N/S	M5P tree	0.090	0.068	0.891
	Irradiance, wind speed, module temperature, temperature	N/S	M5P tree	0.086	0.062	0.899
[18]	Irradiance, temperature, total cloud amount, low cloud amount	Cloudy	GA-BP	0.066	0.056	–
	Irradiance, temperature, total cloud amount, low cloud amount	Cloudy & rainy	GA-BP	0.1286	0.1332	–
[19]	Measured power, irradiance predictions, humidity prediction, temperature prediction	N/S	SVM	0.150	–	–
	Measured power, irradiance predictions, humidity prediction, temperature prediction	N/S	SVM-DF	0.135	–	–
	Measured power, irradiance predictions, humidity prediction, temperature prediction	N/S	ANN	0.180	–	–
[20]	Operating voltage, short circuit current, reverse current, series resistance	Sunny	DE	–	0.0494	–
	Operating voltage, short circuit current, reverse current, series resistance	Sunny	PSO	–	0.0460	–
	Operating voltage, short circuit current, reverse current, series resistance	Sunny	ECSS	–	0.0345	–
	Operating voltage, short circuit current, reverse current, series resistance	Cloudy	DE	–	0.0118	–
	Operating voltage, short circuit current, reverse current, series resistance	Cloudy	PSO	–	0.0112	–
	Operating voltage, short circuit current, reverse current, series resistance	Cloudy	ECSS	–	0.0065	–
[21]	Irradiance, temperature	N/S	GAPSOBP	–	0.0100	–
	Irradiance, temperature	N/S	D-GAPSOBP	–	0.0070	–
	Irradiance, temperature	N/S	GABP	–	0.0100	–
	Irradiance, temperature	N/S	D-GABP	–	0.0073	–

4   Conclusion

In this work, a low-cost Internet of Things system was used to observe the output and context of two modules, one dusty and one clean. The measured data was used to predict the output of a dusty module using only the temperature of the dusty module, the temperature and power output of a clean module, and temporal data. Seven different algorithms were trained and tested. At the end of the evaluation, it was found that the random tree and random forest algorithms were able to predict the output with an RMSE of around 3%, while the output of a backpropagation neural network had an RMSE of around 7%. While the performance is not as good as some of the artificial intelligence discussed in some literature, the simplicity of the design in terms of low financial cost as well as low interference with the modules' circuitry motivates to further pursue the method for large scale farms. It is expected that with a larger dataset and more accurate temperature readings the error rate my drop and the method will therefore prove to be highly efficient in the long run.

Acknowledgment. The research reported here was supported in part by grant #SCRI-18-02, and Petrofac-Chair grant from the American University of Sharjah, UAE.

References

1. Fouad, M.M., Shihata, L.A., Morgan, E.I.: An integrated review of factors influencing the performance of photovoltaic panels. Renew. Sustain. Energy Rev. **80**, 1499–1511 (2017). https://doi.org/10.1016/j.rser.2017.05.141
2. de Freitas Viscondi, G., Alves-Souza, S.N.: A systematic literature review on big data for solar photovoltaic electricity generation forecasting. Sustain. Energy Technol. Assess. **31**, 54–63 (2019). https://doi.org/10.1016/j.seta.2018.11.008
3. Rahman, M.M., Selvaraj, J., Rahim, N.A., Hasanuzzaman, M.: Global modern monitoring systems for PV based power generation: a review. Renew. Sustain. Energy Rev. **82**, 4142–4158 (2018). https://doi.org/10.1016/j.rser.2017.10.111
4. Yang, L., Gao, X., Lv, F., Hui, X., Ma, L., Hou, X.: Study on the local climatic effects of large photovoltaic solar farms in desert areas. Sol. Energy **144**, 244–253 (2017). https://doi.org/10.1016/j.solener.2017.01.015
5. Maghami, M.R., Hizam, H., Gomes, C., Radzi, M.A., Rezadad, M.I., Hajighorbani, S.: Power loss due to soiling on solar panel: a review. Renew. Sustain. Energy Rev. **59**, 1307–1316 (2016). https://doi.org/10.1016/j.rser.2016.01.044
6. Burton, P.D., Boyle, L., Griego, J.J.M., King, B.H.: Quantification of a minimum detectable soiling level to affect photovoltaic devices by natural and simulated soils. IEEE J. Photovoltaics **5**, 1143–1149 (2015). https://doi.org/10.1109/JPHOTOV.2015.2432459
7. Burton, P.D., King, B.H.: Determination of a minimum soiling level to affect photovoltaic devices. In: 2014 IEEE 40th Photovoltaic Specialist Conference (PVSC), pp. 0193–0197 (2014). https://doi.org/10.1109/PVSC.2014.6925529
8. Pulipaka, S., Kumar, R.: Analysis of soil distortion factor for photovoltaic modules using particle size composition. Sol. Energy **161**, 90–99 (2018). https://doi.org/10.1016/j.solener.2017.11.041
9. Figgis, B., Ennaoui, A., Ahzi, S., Rémond, Y.: Review of PV soiling particle mechanics in desert environments. Renew. Sustain. Energy Rev. **76**, 872–881 (2017). https://doi.org/10.1016/j.rser.2017.03.100

10. Figgis, B., et al.: Investigation of factors affecting condensation on soiled PV modules. Sol. Energy **159**, 488–500 (2018). https://doi.org/10.1016/j.solener.2017.10.089
11. Ilse, K.K., et al.: Comprehensive analysis of soiling and cementation processes on PV modules in Qatar. Solar Energy Mater. Solar Cells **186**, 309–323 (2018). https://doi.org/10.1016/j.solmat.2018.06.051
12. Javed, W., Guo, B., Figgis, B.: Modeling of photovoltaic soiling loss as a function of environmental variables. Sol. Energy **157**, 397–407 (2017). https://doi.org/10.1016/j.solener.2017.08.046
13. Coskun, C., Toygar, U., Sarpdag, O., Oktay, Z.: Sensitivity analysis of implicit correlations for photovoltaic module temperature: a review. J. Clean. Prod. **164**, 1474–1485 (2017). https://doi.org/10.1016/j.jclepro.2017.07.080
14. Salari, A., Hakkaki-Fard, A.: A numerical study of dust deposition effects on photovoltaic modules and photovoltaic-thermal systems. Renew. Energy **135**, 437–449 (2019). https://doi.org/10.1016/j.renene.2018.12.018
15. Shapsough, S., Takrouri, M., Dhaouadi, R., et al.: Using IoT and smart monitoring devices to optimize the efficiency of large-scale distributed solar farms. Wirel. Netw. (2018). https://doi.org/10.1007/s11276-018-01918-z
16. Shapsough, S., Dhaouadi, R., Zualkernan, I.: Using linear regression and back propagation neural networks to predict performance of soiled PV modules. Presented at the 9th International Conference on Sustainable Energy Information Technology (SEIT), Halifax, Canada, August 2019
17. Benhmed, K., et al.: PV power prediction in Qatar based on machine learning approach. In: 2018 6th International Renewable and Sustainable Energy Conference (IRSEC), pp. 1–4 (2018). https://doi.org/10.1109/IRSEC.2018.8702880
18. Meng, X., Xu, A., Zhao, W., Wang, H., Li, C., Wang, H.: A new PV generation power prediction model based on GA-BP neural network with artificial classification of history day. In: 2018 International Conference on Power System Technology (POWERCON), pp. 1012–1017 (2018). https://doi.org/10.1109/POWERCON.2018.8601567
19. Buwei, W., Jianfeng, C., Bo, W., Shuanglei, F.: A solar power prediction using support vector machines based on multi-source data fusion. In: 2018 International Conference on Power System Technology (POWERCON), pp. 4573–4577 (2018). https://doi.org/10.1109/POWERCON.2018.8601672
20. Huang, C., Huang, Y., Yang, S., Huang, K., Chen, S.: Parameter estimation and power prediction for PV power generation using a multi-agent algorithm. In: 2019 IEEE International Conference on Industrial Technology (ICIT), pp. 679–684 (2019). https://doi.org/10.1109/ICIT.2019.8755090
21. Li, J., Wang, R., Zhang, T., Zhang, X., Liao, T.: Predicating photovoltaic power generation using an improved hybrid heuristic method. In: 2016 Sixth International Conference on Information Science and Technology (ICIST), pp. 383–387 (2016). https://doi.org/10.1109/ICIST.2016.7483443

Customized Attack Detection Under Power Industrial Control System

Bin Wang[1], Ling He[1], Huiting Yang[1], Feng Li[1], and Jie Fan[2(⊠)]

[1] State Grid XinJiang Electric Power Co. Ltd., Electric Power Research Institute,
Xinjiang, China
331657859@qq.com, 355080044@qq.com, 731613043@qq.com, 252491552@qq.com
[2] Global Energy Interconnection Research Institute Co. Ltd., Nanjing, China
fanjie@geiri.sgcc.com.cn

Abstract. With the rapid development of information technology, the power system already has the typical characteristics of the information physical fusion system. The power industrial control system is widely used in the power industry. While improving the efficiency, the economic benefits have also been greatly improved. However, the dependence on information technology has also increased the vulnerability to malicious attacks. Power industry control system is facing a more serious threat. In this paper, we combine anomaly detection and data dimensionality reduction to propose a feature extraction method for iForest power measurement data, which not only ensures the targeting of attack detection in the data processing stage, but also takes into account the data quality of feature extraction. In addition, we use deep learning techniques to identify attack behavior characteristics and use captured features to detect attack behavior in real time. We prove the availability of the method through simulation of the IEEE 118-bus power systems.

Keywords: Power industrial control system · Deep learning · iForest

1 Introduction

With the deep integration of informatization and the rapid development of the Internet of Things, more and more information technology is applied to the industrial field, and the power industrial control system is facing the threat of cyber attacks [1].

The power industry control system is an important part of the country's critical infrastructure, covering power monitoring systems such as power plants, substations, and distribution automation systems [2]. However, the existing security protection methods cannot meet the new trend of intelligent and interactive development of industrial control systems [3–5]. Some provincial power companies have begun to introduce new methods and ideas in some production processes to build an industrial control system security system, forming a complete

Supported by organization State Grid XinJiang Electric Power Co. Ltd., Electric Power Research Institute.

D.-J. Deng et al. (Eds.): SGIoT 2019, LNICST 324, pp. 96–106, 2020.
https://doi.org/10.1007/978-3-030-49610-4_8

set of security early warning mechanisms for industrial control systems. However, in order to fundamentally solve the problem of network security of power industrial control systems, it is necessary to model for network intrusion and attack behavior [6]. It is also necessary to combine the operational characteristics of the power industrial control system to build a well-featured network intrusion behavior signature database.

The research on network intrusion of power industrial control system is divided into two aspects [7]. One is for the typical vulnerabilities in the power industrial control protocol, and the other is to analyze the types of industrial control protocols involved in the business in combination with the business scenario. Among them, the threat of attack is a possible factor or event that has potential damage to the organization or assets. Generally speaking, the attack methods for power industrial control systems, including distributed data tampering, forgery control commands, and other advanced and customized attacks closely integrated with business logic, have strong concealment and complexity [8,9].

In 2009, Yao Liu et al. [10] first proposed the basic concepts and related theories of False Data Injection Attacks (FDIA) and conducted simulation experiments. Literature [11–13] studied how to launch FDIA attacks through local parameter information of local power systems. In addition to FDIA attacks based on DC power systems, literature [14] studied the false data injection attacks based on AC power systems. The above research is mainly aimed at the false data attack in static state estimation. Literature [15] studied the false data attack in the dynamic Kalman filter algorithm, proposed an effective attack model, and analyzed the impact of the attack on the state estimation result.

In this paper, we comprehensively consider the above situation, combine anomaly detection and data dimensionality reduction, and propose a feature extraction method for iForest power measurement data. It not only ensures the targeting of attack detection in the data processing stage, but also takes into account the data quality of feature extraction [16]. In addition, we use deep learning techniques to identify attack behavior characteristics and use captured features to detect attack behavior in real time. The main contributions of this paper are listed as follows.

- We use the advantages of isolated forest (iForest) and local linear embedding (LLE) in anomaly detection and data dimensionality reduction, and innovatively combine abnormal score extraction and data dimensionality reduction.
- We design a real-time Deep Learning Based Identification (DLBI) based on deep learning mechanism to detect false data bypassing the traditional bad data detection mechanism.
- In response to our proposed false data attack detection mechanism, we conduct a simulation experiment. Then we compare them with ANN-based and SVM-based false data attack detection mechanisms to test the detection accuracy and efficiency.

The remainder of this paper is organized as follows. In Sect. 2, we briefly introduce a unified preprocessing method for power measurement data. In Sect. 3, we introduce an attack detection mechanism based on deep learning. In Sect. 4, we deploy IEEE 118-bus system in the environment and carry out simulation experiments. Finally, in Sect. 5, we conclude this work and make plans for the future.

2 Uniform Preprocessing of Measurement Data

In this section, we consider that the power system, especially the large complex network, has a high measurement data dimension and the data structure is mostly non-linear. Although the linear dimension reduction method is simple to implement, the effect is not good [17]. At the same time, the individual data dimension reduction will ignore the change of data distribution and abnormal characteristics after the injection attack, resulting in the lack of pertinence of feature extraction [18]. Therefore, we propose an abnormal score extraction method based on Isolation Forest (iForest) as an independent feature, and then use the nonlinear feature extraction scheme of Locally Linear Embedding (LLE).

2.1 Outlier Extraction Based on Isolated Forest

A well-designed false data injection attack can successfully evade the state estimation detection mechanism and invalidate the traditional anomaly detection algorithm. In addition, the power measurement data is increasing rapidly and is already in the category of big data. If we directly use clustering and correlation algorithms to detect abnormal data, it will generate a huge amount of computation, and real-time and accuracy cannot be guaranteed. Based on the iForest algorithm, this paper establishes the iForest anomaly score equation of physical data to realize the feature extraction of the physical system. It has the characteristics of shorter calculation time and higher detection stability, and is suitable for large-scale and high-complexity power measurement data, which meets the requirement of all-weather real-time performance of attack detection.

Building iTree and iForest For the power measurement data set D_p containing n data samples x and φ features f, the establishment of iForest is composed of multiple isolated trees iTree. As a random binary tree, the establishment process of iTree is as follows:

Step1: Select a feature P randomly from the power measurement data set D_p;

Step2: Randomly selecting a single value Q in feature P;

Step3: According to the feature P, binary log segmentation is performed for each record. If any record in the attribute P is $R < Q$, the record is placed in the left child node, and if $R \geq Q$, it is placed on the right child node;

Step4: Recursively construct the left child node and the right child node to construct a binary tree until each sample is isolated or the height of the tree reaches a defined height to form an iTree.

Isolated Forest iForest consists of a large number of iTree trees. The establishment process is a random sampling process. The establishment process is to sample the measurement data set D_p multiple times, and obtain a plurality of sub data sets, and respectively establish multiple iTree according to the sub data sets to form iForest.

Output Outlier Feature After the establishing of iTree and iForest, the abnormal score of each measurement data can be output. For a power measurement data sample x, the calculation principle of the abnormal score is the average traversal depth of all iTrees. For the quantification of the detection sample x at each iTree traversal depth, define the following anomaly score quantization equation:

$$c(\mu) \begin{cases} 2H(\mu - 1) - (2(\mu - 1)/n), & \mu > 2 \\ 1, & \mu = 2 \\ 0, & \mu < 2 \end{cases} \tag{1}$$

$$H(t) = \ln(t) + \xi \tag{2}$$

The iForest exception score for each physical data x can be expressed as:

$$iscore(x) = 2^{\frac{-E[h(x)]}{.c(\mu)}}, \tag{3}$$

where ξ is the Euler constant, $h(x)$ is the path length of x, that is, the sum from the root node to the edge of the isolated node, and $E[h(x)]$ is the mean of the path lengths on all iTrees. When iscore(x) approaches 0.5, the higher the normality, the higher the degree of abnormality when it tends to 1. In the detection of false data injection attacks, we use the abnormal score iscore(x), which is quantized by outliers, as an independent feature of attack detection. The power measurement data after extracting the abnormal score still has high latitude and strong noise. The problem requires further feature extraction.

2.2 Power Measurement Data Dimensionality Reduction Method

After extracting the abnormal score of the measured data in the previous section, it is regarded as an independent feature, and further data reduction is needed for the high-dimensional measurement data. In this paper, we use nonlinear local linear embedding and linear principal component analysis to measure feature data.

Nonlinear Local Linear Embedding. Local linear embedding (LLE) is an unsupervised dimensionality reduction method for nonlinear structural data. For global nonlinear structures, LLE considers each data point in its neighboring data points in a local linear structure, constructing a local reconstruction weight matrix. While maintaining the nonlinear structure of the global high-dimensional space, the low-dimensional mapping of high-dimensional data is sought to achieve data dimensionality reduction. The implementation process is as follows:

(1) In the original high-dimensional data, for each data point x_i, artificially specify the nearest k $(k < N)$ points as the neighboring points, and calculate the distance between x_i and the adjacent points in turn, as follows:

$$d_{ij} = \sqrt{\sum (x_{ik} - x_{jk})^2} \tag{4}$$

(2) Define the local reconstruction weight matrix W. In each local range, the sample point and the adjacent point can be approximated as a linear structure, then there is an error $P(W)$, and the following objective function is established to minimize the error:

$$\min P(W) = \sum_{i=1}^{N} \left| x_i - \sum_{j=1}^{k} w_{ij} x_{ij} \right|^2, \\ j = (1, 2, \cdots, k) \tag{5}$$

where x_{ij} is the neighboring point of x_i, Wij is the weight between the sample points, and satisfies $\sum_{j=1}^{k} w_{ij} = 1$. The error for any point x_i is:

$$e = \left| x_i - \sum_{j=1}^{k} w_{ij} x_{ij} \right|^2 = \left| \sum_{j=1}^{k} w_{ij} (x_i - x_j) \right|^2 = \sum_{j=1}^{k} \sum_{m=1}^{k} w_{ij} w_{in} Q_{jm}^i \tag{6}$$

$$Q_{jm}^i = (x_i - x_j)^T (x_i - x_m) \tag{7}$$

Using the Lagrangian multiplier method, we obtain the following partial reconstruction weight matrix:

$$w_{ij} = \frac{\sum_{m=1}^{k} (Q^i)_{jm}^{-1}}{\sum_{p=1}^{k} \sum_{q=1}^{k} (Q^i)_{pq}^{-1}} \tag{8}$$

When Q^i is a singular matrix, regularize it:

$$Q^i = Q^i + rI, \tag{9}$$

where r is the regularization parameter and I is the identity matrix.

(3) Define the data points x_i and x_j in the high-dimensional space, and find the y_i and y_j projected to the low-dimensional space. The local weight matrix Wij remains unchanged to maintain the nonlinear structure of the high-dimensional space. The following objective function is established:

$$\min P(Y) = \sum_{i=1}^{N} \left| y_i - \sum_{j=1}^{k} w_{ij} y_{ij} \right|^2 = \sum_{i=1}^{N} \sum_{j=1}^{N} M_{ij} y_i^T y_j \tag{10}$$

Among them, the definition of M is as follows:

$$M = (I - W)^T (I - W) \tag{11}$$

At the same time, the objective function satisfies the following:

$$\begin{cases} \sum_{i=1}^{N} y_i = 0 \\ \frac{1}{N} \sum_{i=1}^{N} y_i y_i^T = I \end{cases} \tag{12}$$

Using the Lagrange multiplier method, we get:

$$MY^T = \lambda Y^T \tag{13}$$

As shown in the above formula, the solution of the high dimensional space in the low dimensional space can be obtained by means of feature decomposition, wherein the low dimensional solution Y is the eigenvector corresponding to the smallest eigenvalue in the M matrix.

iForest-LLE Feature Extraction Method. The feature data extraction for the false data injection attack, using the iForest method to extract the abnormal score, can detect most of the random tampering and part of the injection attack in the measured data. However, the well-designed false data injection attack will bypass the traditional state estimation of bad data identification. Therefore, it is necessary to further determine whether or not FDIAs are accepted by the machine learning classification method. This requires further data reduction for high-dimensional nonlinear power measurement data.

This paper combines the advantages of iForest in dealing with anomaly detection and LLE in dealing with dimensionality reduction of high-dimensional data attributes, and proposes the iForest-LLE power measurement data feature extraction method for false data injection attack detection. Figure 1 shows the algorithm flow.

For the power measurement data x, first extract the abnormal score iscore(x) of each data and use it as an independent feature, and then use LLE to perform dimensionality reduction on the high-dimensional measurement data with the specified dimension r. When the attack detection is performed, two characteristics are comprehensively calculated to perform classification decision, thereby defining the attack detection measurement data feature P:

$$P = [ID, iscore(x), f_1, f_2, \cdots, f_r], \tag{14}$$

where ID is the data sample number and iscore(x) is the iForest exception score, $[f_1, f_2, \cdots, f_r]$ is a new attribute of the power measurement data based on LLE dimension reduction.

3   Attack Detection Based on Deep Learning

In this section, we propose a false data detection mechanism based on deep learning mechanism (Deep Learning Based Identification (DLBI)) to detect spurious data that bypasses traditional bad data detection mechanisms [19].

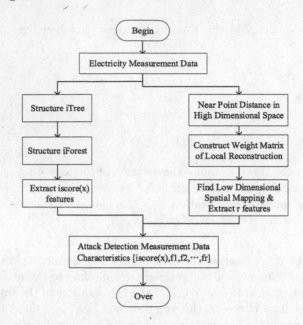

Fig. 1. The iForest-LLE feature extraction method.

3.1   DLBI Detection Method Design

The detection method flow is shown in Fig. 2. The proposed detection mechanism is mainly composed of the traditional State Data Estimator (SVE) and the Deep Learn Based Identification (DLBI) scheme [20]. As described in Eq. (15), the traditional bad data detection compares the critical value with the real-time data, and when the processing result exceeds the critical value ($n > \tau$), the attack alarm is triggered, and the collected data is considered to be infused with false data.

$$\begin{cases} \|z - Hx\|_2 > \tau \\ \|z - Hx\|_2 \le \tau \end{cases} \tag{15}$$

When the processing result is within the critical value ($n < \tau$), the obtained measurement data is transmitted to the DLBI for further detection. In theory, the critical value τ should be within an appropriate range [21]. If τ is too small, the robustness of the traditional bad data detection system to environmental noise will be reduced to some extent, which may lead to excessive unobjectionable attack alarms [22]. On the other hand, if the value of τ is too large, it may have a large impact on the effectiveness of the traditional bad data detection system, and it will also cause a large load pressure on the subsequent DLBI system [23].

Based on Eq. (15), the measured value Z_a injected into the attack vector cannot be found by the traditional bad data detection mechanism, as described below:

$$\|z_a - Hx_{bad}\|_2 = \|z + a - H(x + c)\|_2 = \|z - Hx + (a - Hc)\|_2 + \|a - Hc\|_2 \le \tau \tag{16}$$

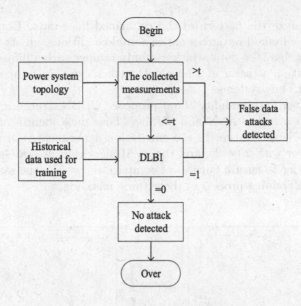

Fig. 2. Attack detection mechanism.

Let $\tau_a = \tau - \|z - Hx\|_2$, if $\|a - Hc\| \le \tau_a$, false data attacks can bypass traditional bad data detection mechanisms [24]. Therefore, we can describe the sufficient conditions for a false data attack to bypass the traditional bad data detection mechanism as follows:

$$a = Hc + t, \tag{17}$$

where H is the measured Jacobian matrix provided to the attacker, c and t are the measured values designed by the attacker, and $\|t\|_2 \le \tau_a$. A false data attack that can be detected by the traditional bad data detection mechanism is called an observable false data attack, and a false data attack that cannot be detected by the traditional bad data detection mechanism is called an unobservable false data attack. In our proposed mechanism, DLBI is used to detect undetectable false data attacks.

4 Experiment Analysis

In this section, we evaluate the performance of DLBI through the IEEE-118 bus test system. In the 118 bus system, the state vector $x \in R^{118}$ consists of the voltage phase angle of each individual bus, and the measurement vector $z \in R^{490}$ consists of the measured values of the bus and the branch that are actually injected into the power system. In our simulation, we use complex load curves collected from real-world environments, only a portion of which was verified false data. In order to train enough false data to train the CBDN model in our proposed DLBI mechanism, we use Fourier transform and principal component analysis to analyze the pattern of the confirmed false data. Considering that the attacker has limited resources under actual conditions, an attacker who can reasonably launch a false data attack can only tamper with a limited load curve. We assume that an attacker of a false data attack can only tamper with 64 bus of the IEEE-118 bus systems.

In order to verify the validity of our proposed CDBN structure, we compared the mechanism of using ANN and SVM as false data identification with our proposed CDBN mechanism. In the simulation experiment, the ANN consists of a hidden layer with 25 cells, and the SVM algorithm uses a Gaussian kernel function. In order to ensure fairness of comparison, we use the same amount of tag data in the training process of these three methods.

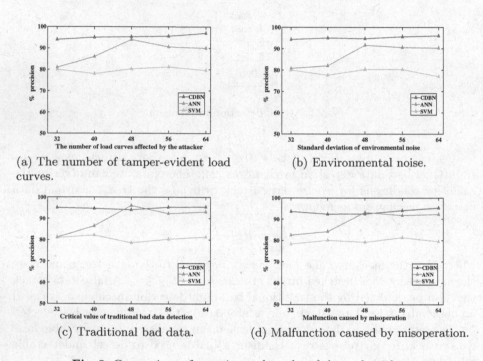

(a) The number of tamper-evident load curves.

(b) Environmental noise.

(c) Traditional bad data.

(d) Malfunction caused by misoperation.

Fig. 3. Comparison of experimental results of three algorithms.

We model the ambient noise as Gaussian white noise $\sim N(0, 0.5)$, set the threshold τ to 10, and consider the number of tamper-evident load curves $k = 32$, 40, 48, 56, 64. Our load curve is made up of 360 samples obtained by collecting power measurements every 4 min on the load bus. From each load curve consisting of 360 samples, we obtain 50 labeled data samples and 200 unmarked data samples for training the DLBI mechanism using CDBN. Figure 3 compares the detection accuracy of ANN-based and SVM-based detection mechanisms. From Fig. 3 we can see that our proposed detection mechanism achieves the highest detection accuracy among three different detection mechanisms. Our proposed test solution has a strong environmental noise robustness. In addition, to a certain extent, it can avoid the detection impact caused by misuse.

5 Conclusion

In this paper, we aim at the problem that the depth of abnormal behavior detection in the power industrial control system is not high enough, and the ability to monitor the customized network attack combined with the industrial control business logic is insufficient. We propose a feature extraction method based on iForest, which realizes high-speed acquisition of real-time data of power industrial control system and unified preprocessing of different structures, dimensions and format data. And we also use the knowledge of deep learning to propose a DBN-based attack detection method to achieve accurate identification of network attacks in specific attack scenarios.

In order to test the attack detection mechanism, we deploy IEEE 118-bus system in the environment and carry out simulation experiments. The final results show that our proposed method has excellent performance.

The future work is mainly to strengthen the integration of power industrial control systems and detection mechanisms, and how to effectively detect advanced and customized attacks that are closely integrated with business logic, including distributed data tampering and forgery control commands.

References

1. Wang, K., Xu, C., Guo, S.: Big data analytics for price forecasting in smart grids. In: IEEE GLOBECOM 2016, Washington, USA, December 2016
2. Wang, X.Z., Ge, Z.Q., Ge, M.H., Wang, L., Li, L.: The research on electric power control center credit monitoring and management using cloud computing and smart workflow. In: 2018 China International Conference on Electricity Distribution (CICED), Tianjin, China, September 2018
3. Wang, Y., Wang, K., Huang, H., Miyazaki, T., Guo, S.: Traffic and computation co-offloading with reinforcement learning in fog computing for industrial applications. IEEE Trans. Industr. Inf. $15(2)$, 976–986 (2019)
4. He, H., Liu, J.D., Jin, Y.K., Li, Z. Zhang, Z.R., et al.: Research on power quality control method of active distribution network with microgrids. In: 2018 3rd International Conference on Smart City and Systems Engineering (ICSCSE), Xiamen, China, December 2018
5. Wang, K., Ouyang, Z., Krishnan, R., Shu, L., He, L.: A game theory based energy management system using price elasticity for smart grids. IEEE Trans. Industr. Inf. $11(6)$, 1607–1616 (2015)
6. Zhang, J., Chen, R., Xiao, L.S., Guo, X.C., Liu, B.: Optimal control for AC and DC power quality of VSC-HVDC. In: 2017 International Conference on Computer Systems, Electronics and Control (ICCSEC), Dalian, China, December 2017
7. Dong, X.M., Sun, H., Wang, C.F., Yun, Z.H., Wang, Y.M., et al.: Power flow analysis considering automatic generation control for multi-area interconnection power networks. IEEE Trans. Ind. Appl. $53(6)$, 5200–5208 (2017)

8. Yu, J., Wang, K., Zeng, D., Zhu, C., Guo, S.: Privacy-preserving data aggregation computing in cyber-physical social systems. ACM Trans. Cyber Phys. Syst. **3**(1), 1–23 (2018). Article 8

9. Wang, Y., et al.: Coordinated recovery strategy of AC and UHVDC interconnected system considering the power grid strength. In: 2017 IEEE Conference on Energy Internet and Energy System Integration, Beijing, China, November 2017

10. Liu, Y., Ning, P., Reiter, M.K.: False data injection attacks against state estimation in electric power grids. ACM Trans. Inf. Syst. Secur. **14**(1), 1–33 (2011)

11. Li, S., Yang, Y.M., Wang, X.: Quickest detection of false data injection attack in wide-area smart grids. IEEE Trans. Smart Grid **6**(6), 2725–2735 (2017)

12. Wang, K., Du, M., Yang, D., Zhu, C., Shen, J., Zhang, Y.: Game theory-based active defense for intrusion detection in cyber-physical embedded systems. ACM Trans. Embed. Comput. Syst. **16**(1), 1–21 (2016). Article 18

13. Liu, X., Li, Z.: Local load redistribution attacks in power systems with incomplete network information. IEEE Trans. Smart Grid **5**(4), 1665–1676 (2014)

14. Yang, L., Ding, C., Wu, M., Wang, K.: Robust detection of false data injection attacks for the data aggregation in Internet of things based environmental surveillance. Comput. Netw. **129**(2), 410–428 (2017)

15. Liu, X., Bao, Z., Lu, D.: Modeling of local false data injection attacks with reduced network information. IEEE Trans. Smart Grid **6**(4), 1686–1696 (2017)

16. Wang, K., et al.: Wireless big data computing in smart grid. IEEE Wirel. Commun. **24**(2), 58–64 (2017)

17. Hug, G., Giampapa, J.A.: Vulnerability assessment of AC state estimation with respect to false data injection cyber-attacks. IEEE Trans. Smart Grid **3**(3), 1362–1370 (2012)

18. He, Y.B., Mendis, G.J., Jin, W.: Real-time detection of false data injection attacks in smart grid: a deep learning-based intelligent mechanism. IEEE Trans. Smart Grid **8**(5), 2505–2516 (2017)

19. Wang, K., Du, M., Maharjan, S., Sun, Y.: Strategic honeypot game model for distributed denial of service attacks in the smart grid. IEEE Trans. Smart Grid **8**(5), 2474–2482 (2017)

20. Ashrafuzzaman, M., Chakhchoukh, Y., Jillepalli, A.A., Tosic, P.T., et al.: Detecting stealthy false data injection attacks in power grids using deep learning. In: 2018 14th International Wireless Communications Mobile Computing Conference, Limassol, Cyprus, June 2018

21. Wei, L., Gao, D.H., Cheng, L.: False data injection attacks detection with deep belief networks in smart grid. In: 2018 Chinese Automation Congress (CAC), Xian, China, December 2018

22. Niu, X.Y., Li, J.N., Sun, J.Y., Tomsovic, K.: Dynamic detection of false data injection attack in smart grid using deep learning. In: 2019 IEEE Power Energy Society Innovative Smart Grid Technologies Conference (ISGT), Washington, DC, USA, February 2019

23. Wang, K., Du, M., Sun, Y., Vinel, A., Zhang, Y.: Attack detection and distributed forensics in machine-to-machine networks. IEEE Netw. **30**(6), 49–55 (2016)

24. Ding, Y.M., Li, K., Meng, Z.X.: CPS optimal control for interconnected power grid based on model predictive control. In: 2018 2nd IEEE Conference on Energy Internet and Energy System Integration (EI2), Beijing, China, October 2018

HomeTalk: A Smart Home Platform

Yi-Bing Lin[1], Yun-Wei Lin[2(✉)], Sheng-Kai Tseng[3], Jyun-Kai Liao[1],
and Ta-Hsien Hsu[1]

[1] Department of Computer Science, National Chiao Tung University, Hsinchu, Taiwan
[2] College of Artificial Intelligence, National Chiao Tung University, Tainan, Taiwan
jyneda@nctu.edu.tw
[3] Graduate Institute of Architecture, National Chiao Tung University, Hsinchu, Taiwan

Abstract. This paper utilizes an IoT platform called IoTtalk to shape "consideration" into a house to make it a smart home. The developed project is called HomeTalk that serves as a platform to accommodate various smart applications in a house. We describe the following HomeTalk applications. The PlantTalk application takes care of house plants. The FishTalk application provides fish comfortable life in the fish tank at home. The BreathTalk application detects the number of people in a room, which also purify the air. The TheaterTalk application uses home and special appliances to create the effects for a 4D experience theater at home. The FrameTalk application allows a painting frame to interact with people in a house. The GardenTalk application provides smart gardening. Then we show how these applications share the sensors and actuators in the house. In the future, we will integrate them through an award winning project called Orchid House.

Keywords: Internet of Things · Smart home applications · Sensor integration

1 Introduction

Victor Marie Hugo said: "Architecture is the great book of humanity". Indeed, the architecture design determines the personality of the house. For example, we may say "consideration is what makes a house a home". This paper utilizes an Internet of Things (IoT) platform called IoTtalk [1] to shape "consideration" into a house. The developed project is called HomeTalk that serves as a platform to accommodate various smart applications in a house. We will describe the following HomeTalk applications: PlantTalk takes care of house plants. FishTalk provides fish comfortable life in the fish tank. BreathTalk detects the number of people in a room and produces fresh air if needed. TheaterTalk uses home appliances to create the effects for a 4D experience theater at home. FrameTalk allows a painting frame to interact with people in a house. GardenTalk provides smart gardening.

In [2], the authors described how to integrate the functionalities of Philips Hue light bulb and Nest Thermostat, as well as other sensors and actuators. The applications are a subset of HomeTalk. In [3] the authors identified the various home automation applications that are also a subset of HomeTalk. Furthermore, the authors emphasized on energy

D.-J. Deng et al. (Eds.): SGIoT 2019, LNICST 324, pp. 107–122, 2020.
https://doi.org/10.1007/978-3-030-49610-4_9

conservation, but did not give any details. The Orchid House of HomeTalk will show how energy conservation can be achieved. In [4], the authors described how to build smart home applications using the FLIP solution [5] based on Arduino Nano [6]. Similarly, the control for HomeTalk is developed through ArduTalk [7] that accommodates Arduino, MediaTek LinkIt Smart 7688 duo, ROHM IoT kit and ESP8266 ESP-12F. Security is an important issue for IoT, which is out of the scope of this paper. In [8], the authors addressed the security issues for smart home. The IoT security management system (SMS) is used to handle a large number of devices [9]. The SMS can also be used in HomeTalk.

This paper is an overview on several IoTtalk-based smart home applications we published recently. The paper is organized as follows. Sections 2–7 describe 6 smart home projects that were already published in journals. All of them are sustainable applications in daily operation. Section 8 outlines how these smart home applications will be integrated in the Orchid House built by National Chiao Tung University (NCTU).

2   The PlantTalk Application

Houseplants give a heartfelt look, which change the atmosphere and feel of the home. They also remove chemical vapors to assist cleaning the air to possibly enhance the living quality. However, to take care of houseplants may be tedious for the home owner. With the IoT technology, plant sensors and actuators can simplify the caring tasks of houseplants. An example is the hydroponic plant box in PlantTalk illustrated in Fig. 1 [10]. In PlantTalk, the actuators are automatically controlled by the sensors. Six sensors and nine actuators are deployed for the plant box.

Fig. 1. The hydroponic plant box

Figure 2 shows the PlantTalk functional block diagram, where the sensors values (Fig. 2 (1), (4), (6), (8), (11), (12), (17), (18)) are read from the input pins of the control board (based on Arduino, ESP8266 ESP-12F, and so on) to the HomeTalk server (Fig. 2 (2)) through WiFi or NB-IoT, and the server gives instructions to the actuators through the output pins of the control board (Fig. 2 (3), (5), (7), (9), (10), (13), (14),(15), (16)).

The pH sensor (pH-sensor in Fig. 2 (1)) indicates the quality of the water. In [10], the optimum pH of the water for misting is 5.5 to 7. When the tap water quality is out of the "sweet spot" pH range, the HomeTalk server (Fig. 2 (2)) activates the Reverse Osmosis (RO) actuator (Fig. 2 (3)) to improve the water quality.

The temperature sensor (Fig. 2 (4)) monitors the room temperature. Most plants prefer a temperature between 60 °F–80 °F. When the temperature is higher than 80 °F, the Fan actuator (Fig. 2 (5)) is activated to cool down the water.

Most plants grow better with a little bit more humidity. The humidity sensor (Fig. 2 (6)) monitors if the air in the room is too dry. If so, the sprayer (Fig. 2 (7)) is activated to mist the plant leaves to increase humidity so that dryness of leaves can be mitigated.

Old water loses oxygen and should be replaced by fresh water. The Dissolved Oxygen (DO) sensor (Fig. 2 (8)) is used to determine if the old water should be drained out by the drain pump (Fig. 2 (9)) and the fresh water should be sucked in by the suction pump (Fig. 2 (10)).

In hydroponic planting, most of the roots should be submerged below water. Therefore we use water level sensor (Fig. 2 (11)) to determine how much water should be added. When the water level is too low, the suction pump is activated.

A software timer (Fig. 2 (12)) is used to trigger the actuators for routine jobs such as nutrition and the photosynthesis process. PlantTalk exercises the Nutrient Film Technique (NFT) where the suction motor (Fig. 2 (13)) pumps the nutrient solution into a grow tray to be absorbed by the plants when the nutrient solution passes through their roots.

For the photosynthesis process, plants need to be exposed to sunlight for at least six hours a day. If the hydroponic plant box cannot access to direct sunlight, light fixtures is required. The software timer periodically activates the white LED (Fig. 2 (14)) for this purpose.

The beauty of PlantTalk is that the plants enhance the air quality of the house through the photosynthesis process. The CO_2 and O_2 sensors (Fig. 2 (17) and (18)) monitors the air quality. When CO_2 is too high, the photosynthesis process is activated by turning off LED-W (white light; see Fig. 2 (14)) and turning on the red light LED-R (Fig. 2 (15)) and the blue light LED-B (Fig. 2 (16)) to speed up the photosynthesis process that transforms CO_2 and water into carbohydrates and O_2. More details can be found in [10].

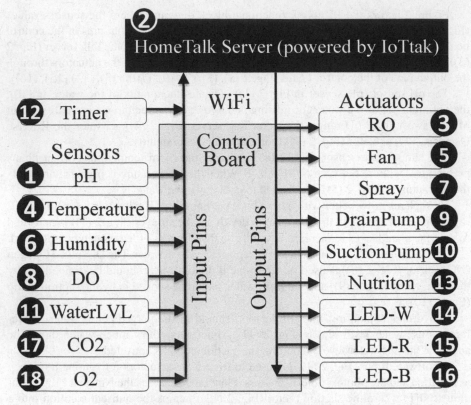

Fig. 2. PlantTalk functional block diagram.

3   The FishTalk Application

A fish tank is a pretty and lively decoration for a house. Watching fish has the calm effects to reduce stress. The IoT technology can further amplifies these effects. For example, a remote food feeder allows the home owner to watch fish feeding at any time in any place. As an example, Fig. 3 illustrates the smartphone display for FishTalk [11], where a camera provides video streaming in the display (Fig. 3 (1)). The camera can be zoomed in and out (Fig. 3 (2)) and moved left and right (Fig. 3 (3)). The dashboard shows all sensor values such as temperature (Fig. 3 (4)) and pH (Fig. 3 (5)). There is also a control panel that allows the user to control the actuators such as the heater (Fig. 3 (6)) and the fan (Fig. 3 (7)).

Figure 4 shows the FishTalk functional block diagram. The temperature sensor (Fig. 4 (1)) monitors the water temperature. For most fishes, the optimal temperature ranges from 77 °F to 80.6 °F. When it is hot, the fan (Fig. 4 (2)) is activated to blow across the surface of the tank water to increase evaporation and therefore cool down the water. When it is too cold, the heater is activated (Fig. 4 (3)) to warm up the water.

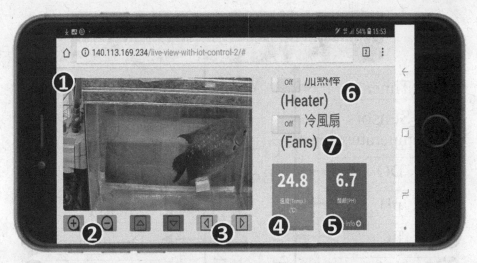

Fig. 3. Viewing the aquarium through the FishTalk display.

Decreased O2 concentration combined with elevated CO2 concentration in the water results in fish suffocation. The Dissolved Oxygen (DO) sensor (Fig. 4 (4)) monitors the dissolved O2 concentration. When it is below a threshold, the air pump (Fig. 4 (5)) is activated to increase the dissolved oxygen in the water.

The comfortable pH level in the aquarium ranges from 6 to 9. The pH value is affected by water hardness, and is also affected by CO2 that acidifies the water. When the pH sensor (Fig. 4. (6)) detects that the pH level is out of the comfortable range, the Reverse Osmosis (RO; see Fig. 4 (7)) is activated to purify the water for the pH level adjustment.

Appropriate Electrical Conductivity (EC) level is essential for fish health. Comfortable EC value ranges from 100 to 300 μS/cm for community freshwater tanks. The EC value is increased due to pollutants. The EC sensor (Fig. 4 (8)) monitors the water quality, FishTalk makes decision on when to activate the drain and the suction pumps (Fig. 4 (9) and (10)) to change the water for reducing pollutants.

The Total Dissolved Solids (TDS) sensor detects (Fig. 4 (11)) anions and cations (such as magnesium, calcium, silicate, sodium, phosphate and nitrate) in the water. When the RO membranes become blocked, the TDS value turns high. When the TDS value is higher than e.g., 40 ppm, it is an early warning for water deterioration, and we should clean or replace the RO membranes.

The water level sensor (Fig. 4 (12)) monitors the water volume in the tank. When it is below a threshold, the suction pump is activated to add water. Like PlantTalk, a timer (Fig. 4 (13)) is used for routine tasks. For example, the timer periodically turns on the food feeder to feed the fish (Fig. 4 (14)). FishTalk also provides lighting for viewing fish (Fig. 4 (15)).

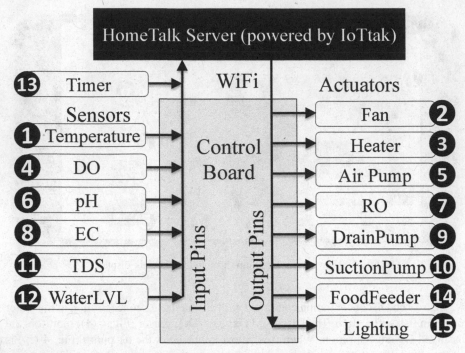

Fig. 4. FishTalk functional block diagram.

4 The BreathTalk Application

Heating, ventilation, and air conditioning (HVAC) [12] are considered items for typical building maintenance. Such maintenance often depends on the number of human occupancy information. In [13] we build the BreathTalk application that utilizes the CO_2 sensors to detect the number of people in a room. The BreathTalk functional block diagram is illustrated in Fig. 5.

In this application, the indoor CO_2 sensor (Fig. 5 (1)) is used to detect the number of people in real time. An outdoor CO_2 sensor (Fig. 5 (2)) is also used as a reference point. The counting prediction is achieved by a machine learning module that includes kNN, decision tree and random forests. In [13] we subtly implemented the machine learning module as a cyber sensor and a cyber actuator. The cyber actuator is called Features (Fig. 5 (3)) that receives the indoor and the outdoors CO_2 values as the features of the machine learning algorithms. The cyber sensor (Fig. 5 (4)) sends out the prediction results to the Display (Fig. 5 (5)). Figure 6 shows the time series for the indoor and the outdoor CO_2 reported in [13]. The figure also shows the predicted numbers of people as well as the ground truth. We note that if we use the indoor CO_2 sensor as the only feature to the AI model, the accuracy of prediction is less than 90%. By adding the outdoor CO_2 sensor as the reference feature, the accuracy of prediction is 96.5%, which is better than the previous known results.

Besides counting people, when the CO2 concentration is high, BreathTalk automatically winds up the curtain (Fig. 5 (6) and Fig. 7 (1)) and opens the window (Fig. 5 (7) and Fig. 7 (2)).

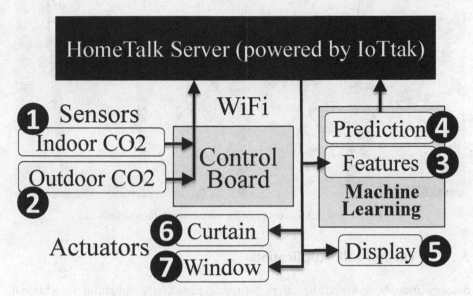

Fig. 5. BreathTalk functional block diagram.

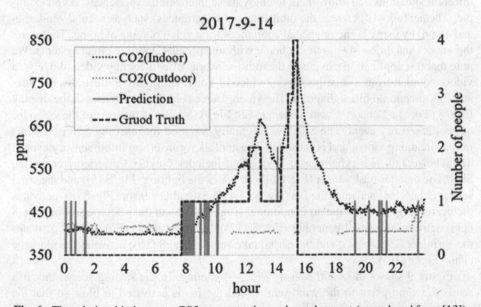

Fig. 6. The relationship between CO2 concentration and people count (reproduced from [13]).

Fig. 7. BreathTalk control of the curtains and the windows.

5   The TheaterTalk Application

Sensory friendly shows create art performance particularly delightful for children. Specifically, the shows generate sensitivity to sensory inputs that expose children to different situations and allow them to enjoy these interesting experiences. As an example, TheaterTalk [14] creates the multi-sensory experiences (such as scents, wind, rain and so on) by using home or special appliances for a video playing at home. Therefore, the viewer can enjoy 4D movies at home without special 4D movie effect systems. We note that this application can create the multi-sensorial effects for any video film, e.g., a video recorded from a smartphone or a video in YouTube. Figure 8 illustrates the TheaterTalk functional block diagram. The video source (Fig. 8 (1)) streams to the display (Fig. 8 (2)). The Sensory Event System (SES; Fig. 8 (3)) marks the time of the video for a specific sensory event. The SES was originally designed for inserting advertisements into a streaming video, and is reused in TheaterTalk for inserting multi-sensory events. The TheaterTalk is a cyber sensor device that includes 6 cyber sensors driven by the SES. The thunder flash sensor (Fig. 8 (4)) activates the lighting (Fig. 8 (5)) and the wind sensor (Fig. 8 (6)) activates the fan (Fig. 8 (7)). The weather sensor (Fig. 8 (8)) activates the heater (Fig. 8 (9)) or the air conditioner (Fig. 8 (10)) and the perfume sensor (Fig. 8 (11)) activates the smell generator (Fig. 8 (12)). The rain gauge (Fig. 8 (13)) activates the sprinkler (Fig. 8 (14)) and the earthquake sensor (Fig. 8 (15)) activates the massage chair (Fig. 8 (16)).

Figure 9 shows the multi-sensory video streaming. In the surfing scene, the SES sends the wind event to the wind sensor, and the fan is activated to blow so that the viewer feels the wind effect. The signaling path is ((3)->(6)->HomeTalk server->(7) in Fig. 8).

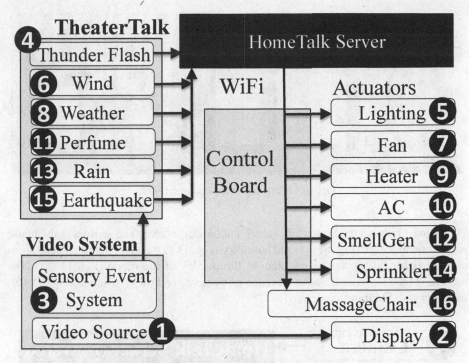

Fig. 8. TheaterTalk functional block diagram.

Fig. 9. Video streaming with multi-sensory effect.

6 The FrameTalk Application

As another sensory friendly show, the FrameTalk application [15] allows a smart frame to interact with the environment conditions at home. In Fig. 10, when it is a sunny weather, the frame shows Vincent van Gogh's art work "Sunny Day". When the camera detects that a person approaches, the frame interacts with the person through her/his smartphone. For example, by using the gyroscope of the smartphone, the person waves to change the pictures in the frame.

Fig. 10. Interaction with a picture frame.

Figure 11 shows the FrameTalk functional block diagram. The sensors in the house such as temperature (Fig. 11 (1)) and humidity (Fig. 11 (2)) collect the room conditions and the HomeTalk server passes them to the display of the frame (Fig. 11 (3)). The camera (Fig. 11 (4)) detects the presence of persons, and the gyroscope (Fig. 11 (5)) interacts with the frame content.

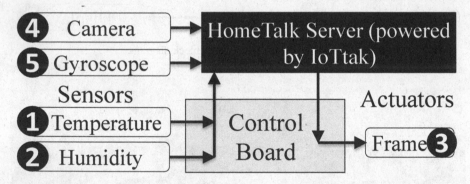

Fig. 11. FrameTalk functional block diagram.

7 The GardenTalk Application

Gardening adds gorgeousness to the yard at home. Besides enjoying of homegrown harvest, a garden provides healthy environment around the house. The IoT technology assists the gardener to handle plant growing. An example is GardenTalk that uses the technology developed in [16] to deploy sensors and actuators in a garden. A micro weather station (Fig. 12 (1)) is deployed with sensors (Fig. 13 (1)–(7)) for CO2, temperature, humidity, atmosphere pressure (AP), the rain gauge, the ultraviolet (UV) and the wind gauge. GardenTalk also deploys soil sensors include (Fig. 13 (8)–(11)) a 3-in-1 sensor for moisture, temperature, and electrical conductivity (EC; see Fig. 12 (2)), and a pH sensor (Fig. 12 (3)). The actuators (Fig. 13 (12)–(14)) include those for irrigation, fertilization and pesticide. The drippers are connected to the irrigation tank (Fig. 12 (4)) and the fertilizer tank (Fig. 12 (5)) to form a drip irrigation system controlled by the pump (Fig. 12 (6)).The pest sprayers connected to the biopesticide tank (Fig. 12 (7)). Like the irrigation system, the biopesticide liquid is sent to the sprayers by the pump.

Fig. 12. The garden with sensors and actuators.

The irrigation drippers are driven by soil moisture sensor, the rain gauge and a timer. When the humidity level is too low, the water is pumped in. We also use the timer (Fig. 13 (3)) to perform routine irrigation when the rainfall amounts lower than 2 mm measured by the rain gauge. The fertilizer drippers are controlled by the EC and the pH sensors (Fig. 13 (10) and (11)). Through these sensor values, GardenTalk calculates the Nitrogen, Phosphorus and Potassium ingredients in soil through the AI module (Fig. 12 (15)) and decides the amount of fertilization. The pest control (Fig. 13 (16)) is more complicate. We used a regression model with temperature (Fig. 13 (2)), humidity (Fig. 13 (3)) and wind speed (Fig. 13 (7)) to create the features for the AI model to determine if the pest sprayer (Fig. 13 (14)) should be activated. The sensors and actuators involve other complex agriculture functions and the reader is referred to [16] for the details.

8 Discussion and Conclusions

Most HomeTalk applications can share same kinds of sensors, although we have not done so for the current implementations described in Sects. 2–7. For example, FrameTalk may interact with all sensors listed in Table 1 with various animation art works displayed in the frame. If the water sources for the aquarium tank and the hydroponic plant box are the same, then most sensors and actuators can be shared by PlantTalk and FishTalk.

In Table 1, the pH sensor in the water can be shared by PlantTalk and FishTalk. GardenTalk needs a separate pH sensor inserted in the soil. The indoor temperature sensor can be shared by PlantTalk and FrameTalk (to display the room temperature). FishTalk may share the same temperature sensor or have a separate one inserted in the water. An outdoor temperature sensor is used by GardenTalk.

The indoor humidity sensor is used in PlantTalk and the outdoor sensor is used in GardenTalk. BreathTalk may use both indoor and outdoor humidity sensors for HVAC. The indoor O2 sensor can be shared by PlantTalk and BreathTalk. FishTalk used DO, the O2 sensor in the water. The water level sensor can be shared by PlantTalk and FishTalk.

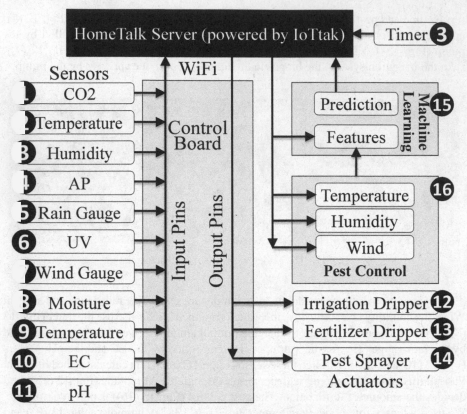

Fig. 13. The GardenTalk functional block diagram.

The indoor CO_2 sensor is shared by PlantTalk and BreathTalk. The outdoor CO_2 sensor is used by GardenTalk and BreathTalk. The software timer with multiple targets is shared by all applications that execute routine tasks. The EC and the TDS sensors can be shared by PlantTalk and FishTalk to detect water quality.

In the current implementations, both BreathTalk and GardenTalk use the AI module. In the future, all applications can utilize AI to do something smart. In HomeTalk, all applications can use smartphones to provide the control panel, the sensor dashed board, and video streaming. The FishTalk smartphone example is shown in Fig. 3, which applies to all HomeTalk applications. Similarly, all HomeTalk applications in a room can share one camera. The zooming and rotating features of the camera in Fig. 3 (2) and (3) can be preset to point to several applications, and the camera automatically moves to the target object (e.g., the aquarium tank, the plant box, the curtains and so on) that the user wants to view.

The sensors in a micro weather station for rain, air pressure, UV, and wind are used in GardenTalk. These sensors can be calibrated with the near-by government weather station. Although the sensor values of the government station and the micro station are not exactly the same, they have some correlations (see Fig. 14) that can be used for calibration. Then the micro weather station's sensors may serve for sensor failure detection at home. For example, we use the rain gauge, the indoor and the outdoor humidity sensors to mutually test if any sensor is out of order. The details will be addressed in a separate paper.

Table 1. Sensors used in HomeTalk

Sensors	PlantTalk	FishTalk	BreathTalk	FrameTalk	GardenTalk
pH	x	x			x
Temperature	x	x		x	x
Humidity	x			x	x
O2	x		x		
Water level	x	x			
CO2	x		x		x
Timer	x	x			x
DO	x	x			
EC	x	x			x
TDS	x	x			
AI module[a]		x			x
Smartphone[a]	x	x	x	x	
Camera	x	x	x	x	x
Rain gauge				x	x
Air pressure				x	x
UV				x	x
Wind gauge				x	x

[a]The device serves as both sensor and actuator.

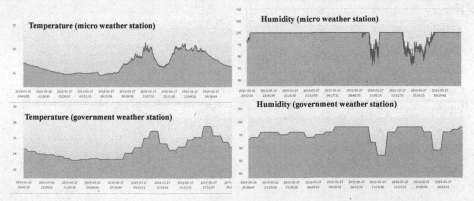

Fig. 14. Sensor Data from the micro weather station and the nearby government weather station.

Table 2 lists the actuators used in the HomeTalk applications. Sharing of actuators is subtle and should be carefully planned. For example, the RO actuator can be shared by PlantTalk and FishTalk to purify water. However, when to activate the RO should be carefully designed. For example, the optimum pH level for PlantTalk ranges from 4.5 to 7. On the other hand, the range is [6, 9] for FishTalk. Therefore, we may activate the RO if the pH level is not in the range [6, 7].

Similarly, the optimum water temperature range is [60 °F, 80 °F] for PlantTalk and is [77 °F, 80.6 °F] for FishTalk. Therefore the fan, the AC, and the heater can be shared to maintain the water temperature in the range [77 °F, 80 °F].

Indoor water spray can be shared by PlantTalk and TheaterTalk but is activated at different times for these two applications. Drain and Suction pumps are shared by both PlantTalk and FishTalk. In "aquaponics", the nutrition of the plants may come from fish excrement. Furthermore, the waste water filtered by the RO outlet contains fruitful ingredients such as nitrates, phosphates, heavy metals, and pesticides that can be reused by the irrigation system of GardenTalk [11].

The curtain is controlled for PlantTalk to get more sunlight. Both the window and the curtain are controlled to get fresh air in BreathTalk, and the indoor blue and red lights are used in PlantTalk to generate fresh air for BreathTalk. The outdoor lighting is

Table 2. Actuators used in HomeTalk

Actuators	PlantTalk	FishTalk	BreathTalk	TheaterTalk	FrameTalk	GardenTalk
RO	x	x				
Fan	x	x		x		
Spray	x			x		x
Drain pump	x	x				
Suction pump	x	x				
Nutriton	x					x
Lighting	x	x		x		x
Heater		x		x		
Air pump		x				
Food feeder		x				
Display				x	x	
Curtain	x		x			
Window	x	x	x			
Air cond.	x	x		x		
Massage chair				x		
Perfume			x	x		
Dripper						x

used by GardenTalk at night. The water dripper used in GardenTalk can be extended to indoor orchid irrigation shown in Fig. 15 (4)).

In the future, we will integrate the smart home applications in NCTU Orchid House that took three big awards in Solar Decathlon Europe 2014 [17]. Figure 15 illustrates the Orchid House sponsored by Taiwan Semiconductor Manufacturing Company Limited. This building was constructed with recycled plastic material for heat storing wall (thermal mass; Fig. 15 (1)) that achieved 97% of plastic recycling. Over 90% of recycled glass was used as heat and sound proof materials (Fig. 15 (2)). The house collects rain water. The water is blown by several large silent fans to cool down the air (Fig. 15 (3)). The cool air is then drawn through the house by a water wall stationed at the opposite end of the house. POLLI-Brick™ made by the recycled plastic bottles is used to fill with water to absorb heat during the day. Radiant heat is released at night. Drip irrigation of GardenTalk is being used for watering the orchids in the wall (Fig. 15 (4)).

Fig. 15. The Orchid House.

Besides the sensors and the actuators in Tables 1 and 2, there are over 50 light sources in the Orchid House. We will study how to use HomeTalk to control the light colors and intensities to create various atmosphere scenarios at home.

:

Author Contributions. Y.-B. Lin: Design of IoTtalk and smart home applications, Y.-W. Lin: Design and implementation of IoTtalk, S.-K. Tseng: Orchid house architecture, J.-K. Liao and T.-H. Hsu: Design and implementation of IoTtalk.

Funding. This research was funded by the Center for Open Intelligent Connectivity from The Featured Areas Research Center Program within the framework of the Higher Education Sprout Project by the Ministry of Education (MOE) in Taiwan, R.O.C., and Ministry of Science and Technology Grant 107R491 and 108-2221-E-009-047.

Conflicts of Interest. The authors declare no conflict of interest.

References

1. Lin, Y.-B., Lin, Y.-W., Huang, C.-M., Chih, C.-Y., Lin, P.: IoTtalk: a management platform for reconfigurable sensor devices. IEEE Internet Things J. **4**(5), 1152–1562 (2017)
2. Pătru, I.I., Carabaş, M., Bărbulescu, M., Gheorghe, L.: Smart home IoT system. In: 15th RoEduNet Conference: Networking in Education and Research (2016)
3. Suresh, S., Sruthi, P.V.: A review on smart home technology. In: 2015 Online International Conference on Green Engineering and Technologies (IC-GET), pp. 1–3 (2015)
4. Malche T., Maheshwary, P.: Internet of Things (IoT) for building smart home system. In: International Conference on I-SMAC (IoT in Social, Mobile, Analytics and Cloud) (I-SMAC), pp. 65–70 (2017)
5. Frugal Labs Tech Solutions Pvt Ltd. (2019). https://frugal-labs.com
6. Arduino, N. (2019). http://www.arduino.cc
7. Lin, Y.-W., Lin, Y.-B., Yang, M.-T., Lin, J.-H.: ArduTalk: an Arduino network application development platform based on IoTtalk. IEEE Syst. J. **13**(1), 468–476 (2019)
8. Erfani, S., Ahmadi, M., Chen, L.: The Internet of Things for smart homes: an example. In: 2017 8th Annual Industrial Automation and Electromechanical Engineering Conference (IEMECON) (2017)
9. Chen, L., Erfani, S.: A note on security management of the Internet of Things. In: Proceeding of IEEE 30th Canadian Conference on Electrical and Computer Engineering (CCECE), pp. 1–4. IEEE (2017)
10. Van, L.-D., et al.: PlantTalk: a smartphone-based intelligent hydroponic plant box. Sensors **19**(8), 1763 (2019)
11. Lin, Y.-B., Tseng, H.-C.: FishTalk: an IoT-based mini aquarium system. IEEE Access **7**(1), 35457–35469 (2019)
12. DOE: Building energy databook. Technical report, US Department of Energy (2011)
13. Lin, Y.-W., Lin, Y.-B., Liu, C.-Y.: AItalk: a tutorial to implement AI as IoT devices. IET Netw. **8**(3), 195–202 (2019)
14. Lin, Y.-B., Yang, M.-T., Lin, Y.-W.: Low-cost four-dimensional experience theater using home appliances. IEEE Trans. Multimedia **21**(5), 1161–1168 (2019)
15. Lai, W.-S., Lin, Y.-B., Hsiao, C.-Y., Chen, L.-K., Wu, C.-F., Lin, S.-M.: FrameTalk: human and picture frame interaction through the IoT technology. Mob. Netw. Appl. **24**(5), 1475–1485 (2019). https://doi.org/10.1007/s11036-019-01269-9
16. Chen, W.L., et al.: AgriTalk: IoT for precision soil farming of turmeric cultivation. IEEE Internet Things J. **6**(3), 5200–5223 (2019). https://doi.org/10.1109/jiot.2019.2899128
17. Taiwan Today (2014). https://taiwantoday.tw/news.php?unit=10&post=20855

Deep Learning Based Pest Identification on Mobile

Yulin Duan[1], Dandan Li[2], and Chongke Bi[3(✉)]

[1] Institute of Agricultural Resources and Regional Planning, Chinese Academy of Agricultural Sciences, Beijing 100081, China
[2] Beijing Agristrong Science and Technology Development Co., Ltd., Beijing 100089, China
[3] College of Intelligence and Computing, Tianjin University, Tianjin 300350, China
bichongke@tju.edu.cn

Abstract. Crops, vegetables, fruit trees, flowers and other cash crops, are often harmed by a variety of harmful organisms, plant pathogens, pests, weeds and pest rats, etc. Plant diseases and insect pests often occur, which are one of the main factors which causes the damage of leaves and crop failure. Therefore, in order to stop the pest, it is extremely important to identify the pests of plants and their characteristics correctly. In this paper, an effective and scalable image recognition algorithm is proposed for disease detection. Meanwhile, MobileNets is employed for developing our method on mobile devices. Finally, a dataset consists of three apple diseases is used to demonstrate the effectiveness of our method. In the experiments, transfer learning is used to train a deep convolutional neural network for identifying two types of pest damage, apple rusts and apple Alternaria leaf spot. Our results show that the MobileNets model offer a fast, affordable, and easy-to-deploy strategy for plant disease detection.

Keywords: Pest identification · Deep learning · Mobile

1 Introduction

Diseases and insect pests are one of the main causes of fruit loss, and timely prevention and treatment of diseases is of great significance [1]. However, due to the following problems, it is often difficult to obtain good control effects. (1) The level of cognition of pests and diseases is limited, and it is difficult to obtain expert guidance. (2) It is impossible to grasp the probability and development of surrounding pests and diseases on a larger scale, and it is powerless to make trend judgments. If we just rely on a few experts or insect researchers, through manual inspection and visual observation, the recognition efficiency is low and the recognition rate is extremely unstable. In this paper, we take apple leaf diseases as the research object and proposed a new method for plant diseases classification. Apples often suffer from different kinds of diseases, such as apple rusts and apple alternaria leaf spot. Apple Rusts – Rust usually appears as orange-yellow spots on the leaves, branches, and fruits of apple trees. There are three

D.-J. Deng et al. (Eds.): SGIoT 2019, LNICST 324, pp. 123–128, 2020.
https://doi.org/10.1007/978-3-030-49610-4_10

different forms of rust fungus, including cedar-apple rust, cedar-hawthorn rust and cedar-quince rust. Among these, cedar-apple rust is the most common rust that affects apple trees. Lesions usually occur in late spring or early summer with small, round, purple or black spots on the leaves at first. Then, the diameter of these spots gradually expanded to 1/8 to ¼ inch with a purple border, while some spots turned grayish brown. Most lesions may disappear at later stages. Some lesions may develop secondary swelling becoming irregular and darker, gaining a "frog eye" appearance. In recent years, many studies have focused on convolutional neural networks (CNNs), which have achieved significant results in the field of image classification. Thus, we propose a new apple plant disease classification method based on CNNs. Our method, based on MobileNetV1 [2], which using depthwise separable convolution as efficient building blocks.

The remainder of this paper is organized as follows: Sect. 2 provides the related work on plant disease classification. Section 3 introduces the architecture of MobileNet and the detail of the proposed method. Section 4 describes the experimental evaluation, the results, and how to deploy deep learning models. Section 5 summarizes the paper and the future extensions.

2 Related Work

In the last ten years, a number of work has been done on the classification of plant diseases based on machine learning techniques. These methods can be divided into two categories, including classification by traditional algorithms and classification by deep learning algorithms.

2.1 Classification by Traditional Algorithm

Traditional image classification algorithms include k-Nearest-Neighbor, support vector machines, and BP neural network etc. Moshou et al. [3] proposed a neural network algorithm based on leaf spectral information to monitor wheat yellow rust. Wang et al. [4] used BP neural network for early warning and monitoring of tomato late blight. Rumpf et al. [5] combined support vector machine (SVM) and leaf reflectivity to monitor beet pests and disease symptoms. Sannakki et al. [6] proposed an algorithm for automatic classification of pests and diseases on leaf images, which first analyzes the specific color information of infected plants by pattern recognition technology, separates the infected points, and then classifies them based on fuzzy theory. Xu et al. [7] realized the detection of wheat rust by image edge monitoring technology.

2.2 Classification by Deep Learning Algorithm

Deep learning-based image classification methods include LeNet, AlexNet, MobileNet and ResNet etc. Sladojevic et al. [8] uses deep convolutional neural network to successfully identify 13 pests and diseases from healthy leaves of five crops with an average accuracy of 96.3%. Fujita et al. [9] proposed a four-layer convolutional neural network method to identify cucumber leaf diseases and pests, after four fold cross-validation, recognition accuracy reaches 82.3%. Amara et al. [1] combined LeNet deep learning model with image feature extraction technology to monitor the pests and diseases of two kinds of banana leaves. Picon et al. [10] combined image segmentation and deep convolutional neural network to monitor three common wheat diseases.

3   The Proposed Deep Learning Model for Pest Identification

Convolutional neural network (CNN) is a representative algorithms of target recognition, and there have been AlexNet, VGG, GoogleNet, VGGNet, Resnet and so on. In order to pursue higher accuracy, more deeper network with more parameters and more complex computing structure are constructed. However, once the network incubated in these laboratories is deployed in production practice, it will encounter various unexpected difficulties. For example, computing is inefficient, especially on mobile devices with limited computing resources, such as mobile phones/pads. Suppose we take a picture, and then ask an AI-powered APP to help us identify what's on the picture, and it thinks for more than ten seconds, which is unacceptable efficiency.

In order to combine the power of CNN with specific production practice, and make it more practical and usable, the existing methods can be roughly divided into two categories, including compressed pre-trained networks and directly trained small networks. MobileNet model belongs to the second approach.

The MobileNet is built on depthwise separable convolutions, except the first layer is a full convolutional layer. As shown in Fig. 1, the depthwise separable convolution consist of depthwise layers and pointwise layers, which followed by batchnorm and ReLU. MobileNet has 28 layers. The model introduces two simple global hyperparameters to balance the delay and accuracy effectively. These two superparameters, width multiplier and resolution multiplier, allow model builders to obtain a good balance between model size and accuracy according to the constraints of the problem.

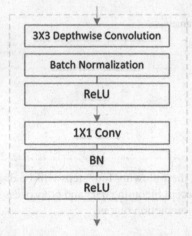

Fig. 1. The structure of Depthwise Separable convolutions.

Fig. 2. Example of two apple diseases

4   Experiments and Discussion

4.1   Experiment Setup

For MobileNet model training and testing, a database containing 1582 photographs of leaves of healthy and infected plants was constructed, which contains three classes of apple leaf diseases (including classes: healthy leaf, alternaria leaf blotch leaf, and rust leaf). These images were collected by the agriculture experts who are visiting and surveying kinds of orchards in Shaanxi Province (see Fig. 2). Table 1 shows the number of original pictures and enhanced images corresponding to different diseases.

To increase the amount of data for training and increase noise data, an image generator was created. With this image generator, we can expand the dataset by randomly rotating, translating, flipping, trimming, and cutting the images. A larger dataset allow us to get better results.

The MobileNets training is done in Tensorflow with the help of asynchronous gradient descent having 10000 training steps. The training parameters of the network were set as Table 2.

Table 1. Dataset of apple leaf diseases.

Apple leaf diseases	Number of original images	Number of processed images
Apple-healthy	126	791
Apple rusts	273	1935
Apple alternaria leaf spot	383	2106
Total	782	4832

Table 2. Hyper-parameters

Parameter	Learning Rate	label_smoothing	moving_average_decay	batch_size	num_clones	learning_rate_decay_factor	num_epochs_per_decay
Value	0.18	0.1	0.9999	96	4	0.98	0.625

4.2   Experimental Results and Discussion

After training the neural network model (Fig. 3), the following four steps will be done in our software (Fig. 4): load the trained model, accept incoming data and preprocess it, predict using our loaded model, and handling the prediction output.

Fig. 3. Representative examples of classifications of testing images.

Fig. 4. Representative examples of mobile interface

5 Conclusions

Due to the threat of various diseases, the apple constant and quality received serious damage. In this work, a mobile pest identification system based on deep learning was proposed. The proposed models are named MobileNets, which is a lightweight neural network model based on depthwise separable convolutions. Then the MobileNets are applied to a wide variety of fruit trees image datasets, and deployed on the mobile phone. Using our proposed method, farmers can enter photos of diseased leaves, and get feedback of the type of the disease in less than 1 s.

In the future, we will test more apple trees diseases with our model, and combine with disease prediction to provide guidance for the protection and treatment of plant diseases.

Acknowledgments. This work was partly supported by the National Natural Science Foundation of China under Grant No. 61702360.

References

1. Amara, J., Bouaziz, B., Algergawy, A.: A deep learning-based approach for banana leaf diseases classification. In: Proceedings of 2nd BigDS Workshops, pp. 79–88 (2017)
2. Howard, A.G., et al.: MobileNets: efficient convolutional neural networks for mobile vision applications, in Arxiv (2017)
3. Moshou, D., Bravo, C., West, J., Wahlen, S., McCartney, A., Ramon, H.: Automatic detection of 'Yellow Rust' in wheat using reflectance measurements and neural networks. Comput. Electron. Agric. **44**(3), 173–188 (2004)
4. Wang, X., Zhang, M., Zhu, J., Geng, S.: Spectral prediction of phytophthora infestans infection on tomatoes using artificial neural network (ANN). Int. J. Remote Sens. **29**(6), 1693–1706 (2008)
5. Rumpf, T., Mahlein, A.K., Steiner, U., Oerke, E.C., Dehne, H.W., Plümer, L.: Early detection and classification of plant diseases with support vector machines based on hyperspectral reflectance. Comput. Electron. Agric. **74**(1), 91–99 (2010)
6. Sannakki, S.S., Rajpurohit, V.S., Nargund, V., Kumar, A., Yallur, P.S.: Leaf disease grading by machine vision and fuzzy logic. In: Proceedings of 2nd International Conference on Signal Processing and Integrated Networks, pp. 1709–1716 (2011)
7. Xu, P., Wu, G., Guo, Y., Chen, X., Yang, H., Zhang, R.: Automatic wheat leaf rust detection and grading diagnosis via embedded image processing system. Procedia Comput. Sci. **107**, 836–841 (2017)
8. Sladojevic, S., Arsenovic, M., Anderla, A., Culibrk, D., Stefanovic, D.: Deep Neural Networks based Recognition of Plant Diseases by Leaf Image Classification. Comput. Intell. Neurosci. **2016**(3289801), 1–11 (2016)
9. Fujita, E., Kawasaki, Y., Uga, H., Kagiwada, S., Iyatomi, H.: Basic investigation on a robust and practical plant diagnostic system. In: Proceedings of 15th IEEE International Conference on Machine Learning and Applications (ICMLA), pp. 989–992 (2016)
10. Picon, A., Alvarez-Gila, A., Seitz, M., Seitz, M., Ortiz-Barredo, A., Echazarra, J., Johannes, A.: Deep convolutional neural networks for mobile capture device-based crop disease classification in the wild. Comput. Electron. Agric. **161**, 280–290 (2018)

Prediction Traffic Flow with Combination Arima and PageRank

Cheng-fan Li[1,2], Jia-xin Huang[1], and Shao-chun Wu[1(✉)]

[1] School of Computer Engineering and Science, Shanghai University, Shanghai 200444, China
{lchf,scwu}@shu.edu.cn, 1204833945@qq.com
[2] Shanghai Institute for Advanced Communication and Data Science, Shanghai University, Shanghai 200044, China

Abstract. Modern traffic network information is similar to the complex network structure in that the links between the sections are quite complex. Therefore, predicting the traffic flow between sections can effectively relieve traffic congestion. To solve this problem, this paper proposes a combined model of Arima and PageRank to predict the traffic flow of each section of the road network. First, the trained Armia model is used to predict the average speed and traffic flow of each section, and then the PageRank model is used to calculate the weight of each section. The product of traffic flow and weight is output as the final result. Through the experiment of highway traffic data in PeMS database, this method is verified to be able to predict the traffic flow of the whole road network.

Keywords: Network structure · Traffic congestion · Armia model

1 Introduction

Traffic congestion not only affects people's life in terms of travel, but also causes economic losses, environmental problems and safety problems [1–5]. Such problems cannot be completely solved only by improving road facilities, so intelligent transportation emerges at the right moment.

At present, there are many models proposed to solve traffic prediction, for example, based on statistical theories, there are chaos theory [6], Kalman filtering method [7] and so on; based on non-linear model, there are LSTM method [8], k-nearest neighbor [9] and so on; based on artificial intelligence method, there are neural network [10], Bayesian probabilistic neuron [11] and so on; based on combination model, there are RBF neural network, fuzzy c-mean combination model [12] and based on combination of support vector machine and data demising schemes [13].

The above methods aim at single point prediction and cannot meet the prediction of traffic flow between each section of the road network. In this paper, considering the shortcomings of the existing prediction models, a combined model of Arima and PageRank is proposed to realize the prediction of the traffic flow of the whole network. First, the combined model can predict the traffic flow of each section of the road network.

© ICST Institute for Computer Sciences, Social Informatics and Telecommunications Engineering 2020
Published by Springer Nature Switzerland AG 2020. All Rights Reserved
D.-J. Deng et al. (Eds.): SGIoT 2019, LNICST 324, pp. 129–140, 2020.
https://doi.org/10.1007/978-3-030-49610-4_11

Secondly, the model can calculate the weight of each section in the road network. Third, this method is beneficial to the drivers to choose the better route. Fourthly, the combined model can also calculate the arrival time between sections. When possible congestion time on the road is predicted, road operators will take corresponding measures to avoid traffic congestion.

2 ARIMA Speed and Flow Prediction Model

ARIMA (p,d,q) is a combination of Autoregressive model (AR), Moving Average model (MA) and difference method (I). In this paper, speed V and flow F are obtained by using ARIMA model. In order to reduce the article length, ARIMA formula was used to derive $V = \{Vm, m = 1, 2 \ldots .m - 1\}$. Vm is the output value and the establishment of the model requires the following three steps.

Step1: The purpose of data smoothing is to transform the non-stationary of data sequence into stationary. In order to highlight the smoothing effect, this paper directly performs visual processing of data, as shown in Fig. 1.

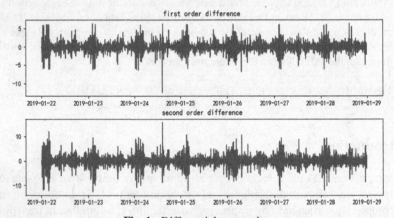

Fig. 1. Differential processing.

As can be seen from Fig. 1, a good stationary can be obtained by applying the second order difference. Therefore, $d = 2$ is set in the model.

Step2: The historical time data of variables are used to predict themselves. However, the premise must satisfy the requirement that the autoregressive model must be of full considerable stationary. AR needs to determine an order p, which means to predict the current value with the historical value of more time in the past. The formula of p autoregression model is defined as Eq. (1).

$$V_t = \mu + \sum_{i=1}^{p} \gamma_i V_{t-i} + \varepsilon_t \tag{1}$$

where type of V_t is the current forecast, μ is constant, p is the order number, γ_i is auto correlation coefficient, ϵ_t is error.

Step3: In order to solve the above AR median error problem, MA is the accumulation of error terms in the autoregression model. The formula definition of q autoregression process is shown in Eq. (2).

$$V_t = \mu + \sum_{i=1}^{q} \varphi_i \, \varepsilon_{t-i} + \varepsilon_t \tag{2}$$

where type of V_t is the current forecast, μ is constant, q is the order number, φ_i is autocorrelation coefficient, ϵ_t is error.

3 PageRank Traffic Flow Modeling

PageRank algorithm [14] is a method used by Google to measure the rank and importance of web pages. The core idea of this method is that the importance of a web page depends on the quality and quantity of other pages pointing to it. At the beginning, assign an initial PageRank value PR to all web pages, which satisfy Eq. (3).

$$\sum_{i=1}^{p} PR = 1 \tag{3}$$

where the formula (3), p is the total number of pages, and then the PageRank value of each page is iteratively and evenly assigned to the page it points to. In order to solve the situation that the pointing page is 0, the page always assigns the PageRank value to itself, sets a scaling factor to reduce the PageRank value of each node, and the network PageRank value is integrated as 1. In other words, the iterative calculation is carried out through the following Eq. (4).

$$PR_{p_k} = \frac{1-\beta}{n} + \beta \sum_{M_{p_k}} \frac{PR_{p_k}}{|L_{p_j}|} \tag{4}$$

where, p_1, p_2, $\ldots$, p_n represents web page; M_{p_k} represents the number of pages p_k linked to other pages; L_{p_j} represents the number of links p_j points to other pages. n represents all pages in the network; PR_{p_k} represents the ranking value of page p_k; Beta represents the probability of the user continuing to browse the page, and the beta usually has a probability value of 0.85.

Therefore, PageRank algorithm can solve the problem of data in the form of graph. A random walk model is established on the directed graph, and then the PageRank value of each node in the directed graph and the contribution value (weight) between nodes are calculated iteratively. Based on this theory, this paper proposes the application of PageRank algorithm in solving the prediction of road traffic. Each section of the road network can be set as a node (the node in the directed graph), and the section and the edge constructed by the section can be set as a path (a sequence passed from one node to another node in the directed graph is called a path), and the sum of the paths is the length. In this way, we obtained the directed graph composed of the road network and the required information (end point, path and length), and then used PageRank for modeling. This paper used PageRank to build the traffic model into the following steps.

3.1 Construction of Directed Graph of Road Network

In this paper, the actual road condition information is modeled and processed, and the road condition information diagram is shown in Fig. 2.

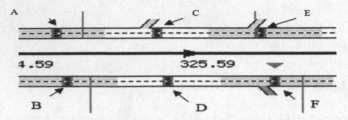

Fig. 2. Road traffic.

As is shown in Fig. 2, road conditions are composed of upstream and downstream. Upstream is composed of section A, section C and section E and the downstream is composed of section B, section D and section F. section A and section F belong to predicted sections. In order to improve the prediction, at the same time, the upstream and downstream traffic flow is predicted in this experiment. The upstream prediction point is A, and the relevant sections are C and E. The downstream prediction point is F, and the relevant sections are B and D. According to the relationship between upstream and downstream sections, the PageRank model is used to construct the upstream directed graph and downstream directed graph, as is shown in Fig. 3 and Fig. 4.

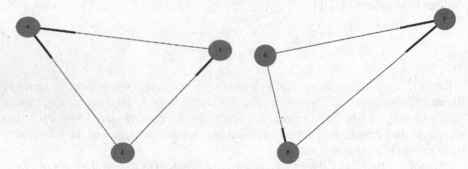

Fig. 3. Upstream directed graph   **Fig. 4.** Downstream directed graph

Figure 3 and Fig. 4 represent the upstream and downstream directed graphs respectively.

The above diagram is explained as follows:

(1) Since upstream E will pass through C and A, when predicting A, it is necessary to consider the influence of point E on its traffic flow at the next moment, influence of point E on its traffic flow at the next moment.

(2) This paper predicts sections A and F, so there is no degree of points A and F. In order to display the road network information more intuitively, the section name is

used to represent the directed graph of the road network by the adjacency matrix, and the matrix of the directed graph of the road network is set as $G = (V, E)$, which has vertices and edges. The adjacency matrix of G has the following properties.

$$A(i, j) = \begin{cases} 1 & \langle Vi, Vj \rangle \\ 0 & \langle Vi, Vj \rangle \end{cases} \tag{5}$$

The upstream adjacency matrix $(V1, V2, V3$ represents $E, C, A)$ is shown in equation

$$\begin{matrix} V1 \\ V2 \\ V3 \end{matrix} \begin{vmatrix} 0 & 1 & 1 \\ 0 & 0 & 1 \\ 0 & 0 & 0 \end{vmatrix} \tag{6}$$

The upstream adjacency matrix $(V1, V2, V3$ represents $E, C, A)$ is shown in equation.

$$\begin{matrix} V1 \\ V2 \\ V3 \end{matrix} \begin{vmatrix} 0 & 1 & 1 \\ 0 & 0 & 1 \\ 0 & 0 & 0 \end{vmatrix} \tag{7}$$

3.2 Build a Random Walk Model on the Directed Graph of Road Network

In directed graph defined on the random walk model representation in the directed graph node to another node state transition, however, and all through the formation of the state transition directed edge constitute an order matrix M, so it calculate the transition probability of between two nodes, the network link between the contribution values of calculation, we will know every specific sections of diversion to other sections of situation by contribution value. Specifically, this paper aims to solve shunting, so the specific steps of solving shunting transfer matrix are shown in Eqs. (8), (9) and (10).

$$F = [f_{ij}]_{n*n} \tag{8}$$

$$f_{ij} \geq 0 \tag{9}$$

$$\sum_{i=1}^{n} f_{ij} = 1 \tag{10}$$

where f_{ij} refers to the node j points to the node i; otherwise, it is 0, I, $j = 1...$ N. According to the establishment of the above directed graph, we can get the upstream and downstream shunt transfer matrix, which is shown in Eq. (11).

$$F1 = \begin{vmatrix} 0 & 0 & 0 \\ 1/2 & 0 & 0 \\ 1/2 & 1 & 0 \end{vmatrix} \tag{11}$$

Similarly, the downstream shunt transfer matrix is shown in Eq. (12).

$$F1 = \begin{vmatrix} 0 & 0 & 0 \\ 1/2 & 0 & 0 \\ 1/2 & 1 & 0 \end{vmatrix} \tag{12}$$

In the table, the vertical axis represents the probability value of branching from other sections, and the horizontal coordinate represents the probability value of between every two sections, which all represent the probability distribution value of the state transition matrix. With this probability value, the distributary ratio between sections is solved. This is a key step in this article.

3.3 The Stationary Probability Distribution Value Is Solved by Power Method

In order to make the probability distribution tend to be stable and ensure the accuracy of the shunt ratio, the solution needs to be solved by power method. The state transition matrix can be expressed as shown in Eq. (13).

$$R = (dM + \frac{1-d}{n}E)R \tag{13}$$

where d is the damped silver and E is the unit vector.

According to the directed graph and diversion and transfer evidence, the PR value in the directed graph of road network can be calculated.

We're going to end up with a stationary probability distribution. In addition, we use formula (14) to calculate the traffic ranking value of each road section (small value means no cars are usually on this road section), and we can choose the travel route according to this traffic ranking value.

$$PR(v_i) \geq 0, i = 1 \ldots 6 \tag{14}$$

$$\sum_{i=1}^{n} PR(v_i) = 1 \tag{15}$$

$$PR(v_i) = \sum_{Vj \in M_{(v_i)}}^{n} \frac{PR(v_i)}{L_{(v_j)}} \tag{16}$$

where $M(v_i)$ represents the node set of v_j, and $L(v_j)$ represents the number of directed edges of node v_j pointing to other road segments.

4   Experiments

4.1   Data Collection

The experimental data in this paper are from January 22 to January 29 in PEMS database. Due to the large number of sections on the road section, six points were randomly selected in the road section for better performance, and the six points were numbered as {a-f} respectively. The speed and traffic data of the six sections are shown in Fig. 5 and Fig. 6.

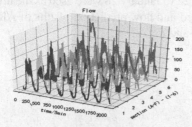

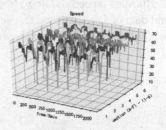

Fig. 5. Speed   **Fig. 6.** Flow

As can be seen in the Fig. 5 and Fig. 6, the data shows periodic changes, which is conducive to the ARIMA model. The following Table 1 shows some of the input data.

Table 1. Input data

5 min	Speed	Flow
1/22/2019 10:35	66.60	99
1/22/2019 10:40	66.70	103
1/22/2019 10:45	67.30	100
1/22/2019 10:50	66.90	124
1/22/2019 10:55	66.30	91
1/22/2019 11:00	64.80	102
1/22/2019 11:05	65.90	122
1/22/2019 11:10	65.20	113
1/22/2019 11:15	65.20	119
1/22/2019 11:20	65.60	95
1/22/2019 11:25	66.50	105
1/22/2019 11:30	65.00	92
1/22/2019 11:35	65.50	98
1/22/2019 11:40	64.60	92
1/22/2019 11:45	66.10	90

As can be seen from Table 1, the data collected on January 22. 5 min is the granularity of data collection; Speed is average Speed; Flow is average traffic Flow.

4.2   ARIMA Model Predicts Results

The Arima prediction model was obtained through the training of historical data, and the predicted values (speed and flow) were used as the input values of the PageRank model. The predicted road sections in this paper are A and F, so the predicted traffic data of each road section in the road network should be obtained before the experiment. Then, according to the PageRank model, the weights between sections were obtained to get the final prediction results.

Traffic data (speed and flow) from January 22 to January 28 were used as the training set and data of Jan. 29 as the test set. The speed and flow prediction results of ARIMA model for the six sections are shown in Fig. 7 and Fig. 8.

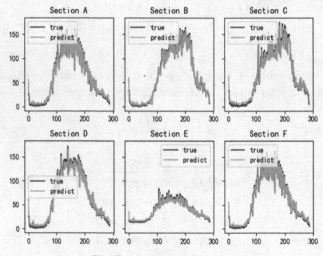

Fig. 7. Flow prediction result

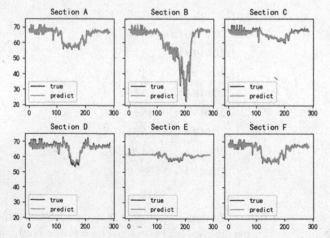

Fig. 8. Speed prediction result.

It can be seen from Fig. 7 and Fig. 8 that the predicted effect is consistent with the actual value.

4.2.1 Evaluation Index of ARIMA Model

In order to prove the accuracy of prediction ability of ARIMA model from the perspective of quantification, this paper introduces three evaluation indexes: average absolute percentage error (MAPE), mean square error (MSE) and R^2 (the closer to 1, the better) to verify the quality of ARIMA model.

The average absolute percentage error, mean square error and regression coefficient R^2 of the three evaluation indexes were calculated in the experiment, and the results are shown in Table 2.

Table 2. The evaluation indexes

Index	MSE(Speed/flow)	MAPE (Speed/flow)	R^2 (Speed/flow)
Results	0.21/0.19	0.22/0.17	0.9/0.98

In summary, it can be seen from the results of the evaluation indexes that the results are relatively good regardless of MSE, MAPE or R^2. Therefore, it can be considered that ARIMA model has a good predictive ability for the experiment in this paper.

MSE residuals of flow and speed are shown in Fig. 9 and Fig. 10.

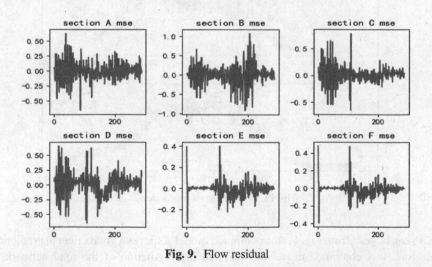

Fig. 9. Flow residual

As is shown in Fig. 9 and Fig. 10, the values of the residuals are relatively small, so it can be seen that the real value and the predicted value are very close, thus verifying the reliability of the model.

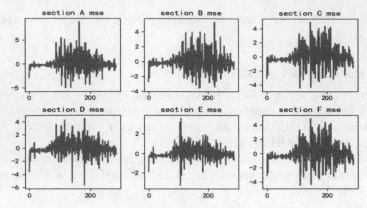

Fig. 10. Speed residual

4.3 PageRank Traffic Flow Prediction Results

4.3.1 Traffic Forecast

The predicted values of segment A and f can be calculated through the predicted values calculated by Arima model and the weights calculated by PageRank model, and the predicted results are shown in Fig. 11.

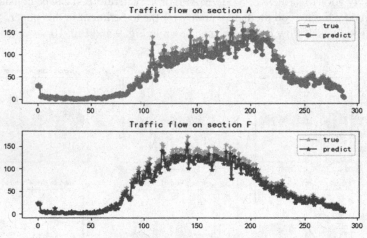

Fig. 11. The result of prediction.

As can be seen from Fig. 11, the combined model achieves a good effect in prediction. Therefore, this combined model has realized the prediction of the road network by utilizing the degree of correlation between sections.

4.3.2 Time Forecast

The velocity V is calculated by ARIMA model, so we can calculate the time T of each road segment to the predicted point by the distance L. The predicted time is shown in Fig. 12.

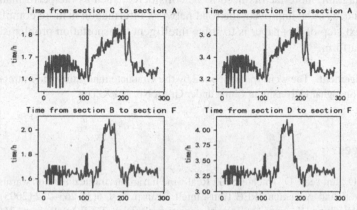

Fig. 12. Time prediction.

$$T = \frac{L}{V} \tag{17}$$

where (17) L represents the length of each section of expressway, T is the time between each sections.

When a certain road is predicted to be congested, road workers can work timely according to the time so as to ease the degree of congestion.

5 Discussions

Different from the existing traffic flow prediction models, a combination method based on Arima model and PageRank model is proposed to promote the whole network forecast. Compared with the traditional prediction methods, the combined model method proposed in this paper improves the prediction accuracy and application. Its value is mainly reflected in the following aspects:

The prediction accuracy reaches 94.7%, which is better than other combined models. Many methods are aimed at single point prediction, but single point prediction has some limitations. Therefore, this method fundamentally breaks through the bottleneck of single point prediction and realizes the prediction of the whole road network. The PageRank model can simulate the road network information map well, for example, the degree of linkage between parts.

6   Conclusions and Future Work

This method not only solves the prediction problem of the whole road network, but also serves as a warning to the road network planning. Therefore, it plays a certain role in solving traffic flow prediction. However, in order to better solve the complex road network diagram, more factors need to be considered, such as the performance of the algorithm needs to be improved, the road network information is more complex and so on. The next step of this paper is to solve intelligent transportation problems based on big data platform.

Acknowledgement. The work was supported by the Graduate Innovation and Entrepreneurship Program in Shanghai University in China under Grant No. 2019GY04.

References

1. Cheol, O., Jun-seok, O., Ritchie, S.G.: Real-time hazardous traffic condition warning system: framework and evaluation. IEEE Trans. Intell. Transp. Syst. **6**(3), 265–272 (2005)
2. Ding, W., Gong, Y., Nan, N.: Toward cognitive vehicles. IEEE Intell. Syst. **26**(3), 76–80 (2011)
3. Wu, C., Zhao, G., Ou, B.: A fuel economy optimization system with applications in vehicles with human drivers and autonomous vehicles. Transp. Res. Part D Transp. Environ. **16**(7), 515–524 (2011)
4. Luettel, T., Himmelsbach, M., Wuensche, H.J.: Autonomous ground vehicles-concepts and a path to the future. Proc. IEEE **100**, 1831–1839 (2012)
5. Grant-muller, S., Usher, M.: Intelligent transport systems: the propensity for environmental and economic benefits. Technol. Forecast. Soc. Chang. **8**(2), 149–166 (2014)
6. Nair, A.S., Liu, J-C., Rileft, L, et al.: Non-linear analysis of traffic flow. In: Proceedings of the Intelligent Transportation Systems (2001)
7. Hua, J., Faghri, A.: Dynamic traffic pattern classification using artificial neural networks. The TRIS and ITRD Database (1993)
8. Wei, W., Wu, H., Ma, H.: An Auto Encoder and LSTM-Based Traffic Flow Prediction Method. Sensors (Basel, Switzerland) **19**(13), 2946 (2019)
9. Davis, G.A., Nihan, N.L.: Nonparametric regression and short-term freeway traffic forecasting. J. Transp. Eng. **117**(2), 178–188 (1991)
10. Dougherty, M.S., Cobbett, M.R.: Short-term inter-urban traffic forecasts using neural networks. Int. J. Forecast. **13**(1), 21–23 (1997)
11. Abdulhal, B., Ritchie, S.G.: Enhancing the universality and transferability of freeway incident detection using a Bayesian-based neural network. Transp. Res. Part C Emerg. Technol. **7**(5), 26–280 (1999)
12. Park, B.B.: Hybrid neuro-fuzzy application in short-term freeway traffic volume forecasting. Transp. Res. Rec. J. Transp. Res. Board **1802**(1), 190–196 (2002)
13. Tang, J., Chen, X., Hu, Z., Zong, F., Han, C., Li, L.: Traffic flow prediction based on combination of support vector machine and data denoising schemes. Physica A Stat. Mech. Appl. **534**, 120642 (2019)
14. Payandeh, S., Chiu, E.: Application of modified pagerank algorithm for anomaly detection in movements of older adults. Int. J. Telemed. Appl. **2019**, 1–9 (2019)

Author Index

Printed in the United States
By Bookmasters